BEST OF THE

Pillsbury

Bake-Off®

desserts

BICENTENNIAL
1807
WILEY
2007
BICENTENNIAL

WILEY PUBLISHING, INC.

Published by Wiley Publishing, Inc., Hoboken, NJ

For general information on our other products and services or to obtain technical support please contact our Customer Care Department within the U.S. at 800-762-2974, outside the U.S. at 317-572-3993 or fax 317-572-4002.

Wiley also publishes its books in a variety of electronic formats. Some content that appears in print may not be available in electronic books. For more information about Wiley products, visit our web site at www.wiley.com.

LIBRARY OF CONGRESS CATALOGING-IN-PUBLICATION DATA

Pillsbury best of the bake-off desserts.
    p. cm.
Includes index.
ISBN: 978-0-471-78720-4 (pbk.)
ISBN: 978-0-470-15177-8 (custom edition)
1. Desserts. I. Pillsbury Company.
TX773.P56 2007
641.8'6--dc22

                                    2006019137

Manufactured in the United States of America

10 9 8 7 6 5 4 3 2 1

Cover photo: Key Lime Cream Torte (page 35)

GENERAL MILLS

Director, Books and Magazines
Kim Walter

Manager, Cookbook Publishing
Lois Tlusty

Editor
Sharon Secor

Recipe Development and Testing
Pillsbury Kitchens

Photography
General Mills Photography Studios and Image Library

Photographer
Chuck Nields

Food Stylist
Carol Grones

WILEY PUBLISHING, INC.

Publisher
Natalie Chapman

Executive Editor
Anne Ficklen

Editor
Kristi Hart

Senior Production Editor
Angela Riley

Cover Design
Suzanne Sunwoo

Interior Design and Layout
Nick Anderson

Photography Art Direction
Lynne Dolan

Prop Stylist
Veronica Smith

Manufacturing Manager
Kevin Watt

Our recipes have been tested in the Pillsbury Kitchens and meet our standards of easy preparation, reliability and great taste.

For more great recipes, visit pillsbury.com

contents

There is nothing like the Pillsbury Bake-Off® Contest.

Have you ever made something so good that you just had to share it? Or tweaked a recipe until it was just right? Or nervously waited as the family took the first bite of a new dish?

Then you've experienced a Bake-Off® Contest.

Like everyday cooks around the country, Pillsbury Bake-Off® Contest winners envisioned making a dish so yummy that family and friends would ask for more.

Of course, the Bake-Off® Contest is a little different. A panel of judges try that first bite. Ninety-nine other cooks share "your" kitchen. But the pay-off for your great recipe is a million times more lucrative than usual.

Whether you're a finalist at a Pillsbury Bake-Off® Contest or simply a star in your own kitchen, you share something special. Both you and Bake-Off® contestants know the food you developed with love for your family will become treasured family recipes in someone's home.

1950s

The first Pillsbury Bake-Off® Contest spurred a phenomenon that many copied but few have perfected over the years. Throughout the '50s, the annual Bake-Off® Contest showcased the creativity of America's best home cooks and their favorite new flavors in the kitchen. The fictitious everywoman, Ann Pillsbury—aka The Pillsbury Lady—presided over the contest and its innovative magazines. The contest showcased kitchen innovations including a white General Electric four-burner, double-oven. By the late '50s, electric mixers, another labor- and time-saving device, were introduced in each cook's "kitchen" at the contest. In the early years, every recipe included Pillsbury BEST enriched flour.

1960s

In the 1960s, the "Busy Lady" was a Bake-Off® theme. Bake-Off® recipes were "shortcutted, streamlined and up-to-dated for you" by Pillsbury. In 1967, the official Bake-Off® magazine featured shortcuts to prize recipes and offered "homemade goodness with hurry-up timing" to the average family cook. At the Bake-Off® Contest, the self-cleaning oven made its debut, and fresh refrigerated biscuit and crescent roll doughs were used as key ingredients for the first time. In 1969, the contest changed forever when it introduced "three divisions"—flour, mix and fresh refrigerated dough—each with a $10,000 Grand Prize. The best recipe won a $25,000 cash prize.

1970s

By 1972, Ann Pillsbury had disappeared from the Bake-Off® Contest, but a new icon had taken her place. The Pillsbury Doughboy, in a cowboy hat, graced the cover of the 1972 Bake-Off® recipe collection. His friendly face would remain a standing symbol of the contest for some time to come. Houston, New Orleans, San Diego and San Francisco were new sites for the contest and reflected America's growing diversity and shifts in population away from the East Coast. Celebrity hosts and judges awarded prizes on Bake-Off® day. In the mid-1970s, the Bake-Off® recipe collection cost around a dollar and included recipes developed for the newest kitchen innovation, the microwave oven.

1980s

In the mid-1980s, the Bake-Off® Contest offered a fast-forward cuisine of quick and easy recipes, snacks and a new entrant to the arena, ethnic recipes. Wontons and Mexican-style recipes popped on the Bake-Off® scene for the first time. The microwave acquired a place in almost every home in the '80s, and many finalists used a microwave to prepare part or all of their entries in a matter of minutes. A microwave category was a new category at the contest. The Grand Prize increased to $40,000, and first-place winners in each of five categories won $15,000 for their favorite family recipes. Celebrities continued to be featured hosts, and in 1983, Bob Barker, longtime host of the TV show *The Price is Right*, awarded more than $130,000 in cash prizes in San Diego.

1990s

Although the theme "quick and easy" had been a staple at past Bake-Off® Contests, for the first time in 1998, Quick & Easy was its own category in the contest, increasing the number of Bake-Off® categories to five. The categories—30-Minute Main Dishes, Simple Side Dishes, Fast and Easy Treats, and Quick Snacks and Appetizers—all reflected the changing nature of the American kitchen. The contest entered the modern era on February 26, 1996, when more than $1,054,000 in cash and prizes were awarded for the first time. The first million-dollar winner was Macadamia Fudge Torte, a recipe developed by Kurt Wait of California, one of 14 men whose recipes were chosen for the contest.

2000s

At the turn of the century, the Bake-Off® Contest turned 50! In the first decade of the new century, the Bake-Off® Contest offered adventurous flavors that blurred ethnic boundaries. For the first time, recipes could be entered in the contest in Spanish. American cooks encountered a variety of cooking styles both at home and in travels around the world. In the 2000s, the number of Bake-Off® categories increased to six. Dinner Made Easy, Wake Up to Breakfast, Simple Snacks, Weekends Made Special, the empty-nest direction of Cooking for Two and a healthy cooking category, Brand New You, reflected a trend set by health-conscious American cooks.

desserts through the decades

Recipes are a reflection of our changing tastes and of our changing times as well. The Pillsbury Bake-Off® Contest entries mark a moment in history that reflects not only "what's for dessert" but what's happening in American homes.

1950s

In early Bake-Off® contests, the one ingredient required for entry was Pillsbury BEST Flour, so it's not surprising that baked goods—specifically scratch cakes—represented the largest category of entries during the contest's first decade. Most women worked in the home and in the kitchen. Homemakers didn't have the kind of access to supermarkets we enjoy today, so most of these early dessert recipes called for ordinary pantry ingredients and were destined as the finale for a dinner party.

Popular '50s Bake-Off® Dessert Recipes

- Orange Kiss-Me Cake
- "My Inspiration" Cake
- French Silk Chocolate Pie

1960s

During the '60s, women led busy lives at home, in their communities and in leisure activities. Women had less time to spare in the kitchen and eagerly turned to convenience foods and time-saving appliances for help. In 1966, the "Busy Lady" theme recognized the growing trend of convenience cooking with simplified recipes. Two products in particular—refrigerated dough and cake mix—were new at the time and both played a role in the Bake-Off® dessert entries during this decade. In 1969, for the first time ever, a dessert recipe made with fresh refrigerated dough (Magic Marshmallow Crescent Puffs) won the Grand Prize.

Popular '60s Bake-Off® Dessert Recipes

- Tunnel of Fudge Cake
- Apple Pie '63
- Buttercream Pound Cake

1970s

"Natural" ingredients were buzzwords during the Bake-Off® contests of the '70s. Homey cakes featuring ingredients like molasses, bananas and oats gained in popularity. There wasn't much happening in the way of pie innovation—in fact, pie baking as a whole was on the decline—but pie-like bar cookies, or "squares," were becoming increasingly common.

Popular '70s Bake-Off® Dessert Recipes

- Nutty Graham Picnic Cake
- Sour Cream–Apple Squares
- Banana Crunch Cake

Hot Buttered Rum and Apple Cobbler (page 98)

1980s

The '80s were the decade of decadence and the Bake-Off® dessert entries from that time mimic this trend. Fancy, indulgent desserts were popular and cooks turned to Europe for inspiration. Pie baking, which had declined during the '70s, was revived with the invention of refrigerated pie crust. Time continued to be a precious commodity and consumers made desserts for entertaining rather than everyday meals. Four of the five Grand Prize–winning recipes of this decade were cakes or tarts.

Popular '80s Bake-Off® Dessert Recipes
- Almond-Filled Cookie Cake
- Apple-Nut Lattice Tart
- Chocolate Praline Layer Cake

1990s

In the '90s, recipes reflected our global community with the most diverse ethnic cuisines ever. Gourmet ingredients became mainstream and cooks displayed increased sophistication by combining the best of European and American traditions. The Chocolate Mousse Fantasy Torte combined an American original—brownies—with a European classic—chocolate mousse. Dessert recipes were inspired by the explosion in availability and variety of products, such as candy bars and ice cream topping. Pies showed a complex exploration and adaptation of U.S. regional favorites.

Popular '90s Bake-Off® Dessert Recipes
- Easy Danish Kringle
- Viennese Chocolate Dream Pastries
- Bananas Foster Tart

2000s

At the turn of the century, technology influenced consumer tastes, and desserts were no exception. For the first time, more than three-quarters of all Bake-Off® recipes were submitted online. Savvy and sophisticated trendsetters reflected major changes in food and culture as Americans enjoyed easy access to the Internet and cable television. At the Bake-Off® Contest, the growth of cooking shows was reflected in artful garnishes on desserts and true "foodie" language previously used only by professional chefs. Banana Dessert Wraps and Greek Walnut Pie represented travelers who ventured around the world but returned home eager to try new ideas with mainstay American ingredients.

Popular 2000s Bake-Off® Dessert Recipes
- Oats 'n Honey Granola Pie
- Raspberry-Crescent Twists
- Pecan Pie–Ginger Cheesecake

country apple cake with caramel sauce

BEVERLY HEALY

Nampa, ID

Bake-Off® Contest 38 • Orlando, 1998

12 SERVINGS

PREP TIME: *15 minutes*

START TO FINISH: *1 hour 35 minutes*

CAKE

2 tablespoons vegetable oil

2 eggs

1 box (15.4 oz) nut quick bread and
muffin mix

3 cups apple pie filling
(from two 21-oz cans)

2 teaspoons ground cinnamon

$^1/_2$ teaspoon ground nutmeg

$^1/_2$ cup chopped walnuts

SAUCE AND TOPPING

$^1/_2$ cup granulated sugar

$^1/_2$ cup packed brown sugar

$^1/_2$ cup butter

$^1/_2$ cup whipping cream

1 teaspoon vanilla

Vanilla ice cream or whipped cream,
if desired

1 Heat oven to 350°F. Spray 13 × 9-inch pan with cooking spray. In large bowl, beat oil and eggs until well blended. Add quick bread mix, apple pie filling, cinnamon and nutmeg; stir 50 to 75 strokes with spoon until mix is moistened. Stir in nuts from foil packet and $^1/_2$ cup chopped walnuts. Spoon into pan; spread evenly.

2 Bake 43 to 50 minutes or until cake is deep golden brown and toothpick inserted in center comes out clean. Cool 30 minutes.

3 Meanwhile, in 2-quart saucepan, mix granulated sugar, brown sugar, butter and whipping cream. Heat to boiling, stirring occasionally. Remove from heat; stir in vanilla.

4 To serve, cut warm cake into squares; place on individual dessert plates. Top each serving with warm sauce and ice cream.

High Altitude (3500–6500 ft): Add $^1/_4$ cup all-purpose flour to dry quick bread mix.

1 Serving: Calories 610 (Calories from Fat 190); Total Fat 21g (Saturated Fat 9g; Trans Fat 0.5g); Cholesterol 65mg; Sodium 330mg; Total Carbohydrate 101g (Dietary Fiber 1g; Sugars 70g); Protein 5g **% Daily Value:** Vitamin A 8%; Vitamin C 6%; Calcium 4%; Iron 10% **Exchanges:** 1 $^1/_2$ Starch, 5 Other Carbohydrate, 4 Fat **Carbohydrate Choices:** 7

taffy apple pound cake

LAVERNE CHENEZ
El Paso, TX
Bake-Off® Contest 21 • San Diego, 1970

16 SERVINGS
PREP TIME: *30 minutes*
START TO FINISH: *2 hours 15 minutes*

10 caramels (3 oz), unwrapped

1 ¹/₂ cups butter or margarine, softened

4 ¹/₂ cups powdered sugar

1 tablespoon vanilla

6 eggs (about 1 ¹/₂ cups)

3 ¹/₄ cups all-purpose flour

2 teaspoons ground cinnamon

1 teaspoon ground allspice

1 ¹/₂ cups chopped peeled cooking
    apples (1 ¹/₂ medium)

Vanilla ice cream, if desired

Caramel topping, if desired

1 Heat oven to 325°F. Generously grease nonstick 12-cup fluted tube cake pan with shortening. With sharp knife, cut each caramel into 8 pieces; set aside.

2 In large bowl, beat butter, powdered sugar and vanilla with electric mixer on medium speed about 3 minutes or until light and fluffy. Add 1 egg at a time, beating well after each and scraping bowl occasionally. On low speed, gradually beat in flour, cinnamon and allspice until well blended. With spoon, stir in chopped apples. Pour batter evenly into pan. Sprinkle caramels over top of batter, separating pieces as needed. Gently swirl caramels into batter with spoon.

3 Bake 1 hour 25 minutes to 1 hour 30 minutes or until toothpick inserted near center comes out clean. Cool cake upright in pan 15 minutes. Place heatproof serving plate upside down over pan; turn plate and pan over. Remove pan. Serve cake warm or cool topped with ice cream and caramel topping.

High Altitude (3500–6500 ft): Heat oven to 350°F. Bake 1 hour 10 minutes to 1 hour 15 minutes.

1 Serving: Calories 440 (Calories from Fat 180); Total Fat 20g (Saturated Fat 12g; Trans Fat 1g); Cholesterol 125mg; Sodium 160mg; Total Carbohydrate 60g (Dietary Fiber 1g; Sugars 37g); Protein 6g **% Daily Value:** Vitamin A 15%; Vitamin C 0%; Calcium 4%; Iron 8% **Exchanges:** 1 Starch, 3 Other Carbohydrate, 4 Fat **Carbohydrate Choices:** 4

almond-filled cookie cake

24 SERVINGS

PREP TIME: *20 minutes*

START TO FINISH: *3 hours 20 minutes*

ELIZABETH MEIJER

Tucson, AZ

Bake-Off® Contest 30 • San Antonio, 1982

1 Heat oven to 325°F. Place cookie sheet in oven to preheat. Grease 10- or 9-inch springform pan. In large bowl, blend all crust ingredients with electric mixer on low speed until dough forms. If desired, refrigerate for easier handling. Divide dough in half; spread half in bottom of pan.

2 In small bowl, mix all filling ingredients. Spread over crust to within $1/2$ inch of side of pan. Between 2 sheets of waxed paper, press remaining dough to 10- or 9-inch round. Remove top sheet of waxed paper; place dough over filling. Remove waxed paper; press dough into place. Top with whole almonds.

3 Place cake on preheated cookie sheet; bake 1 hour 5 minutes to 1 hour 15 minutes or until top is light golden brown. Cool 15 minutes; remove side of pan. Cool completely, about 1 hour 30 minutes, before serving.

High Altitude (3500–6500 ft): No change.

CRUST
2 $2/3$ cups all-purpose flour

1 $1/3$ cups sugar

1 $1/3$ cups butter, softened (do not use margarine)

$1/2$ teaspoon salt

1 egg

FILLING
1 cup finely chopped almonds

$1/2$ cup sugar

1 teaspoon grated lemon peel

1 egg, slightly beaten

GARNISH
4 blanched whole almonds

1 Serving: Calories 240 (Calories from Fat 120); Total Fat 14g (Saturated Fat 7g; Trans Fat 0.5g); Cholesterol 45mg; Sodium 125mg; Total Carbohydrate 27g (Dietary Fiber 1g; Sugars 16g); Protein 3g **% Daily Value:** Vitamin A 6%; Vitamin C 0%; Calcium 2%; Iron 6% **Exchanges:** 1 Starch, 1 Other Carbohydrate, 2 $1/2$ Fat **Carbohydrate Choices:** 2

banana crunch cake

BONNIE BROOKS

Salisbury, MD

Bake-Off® Contest 24 • Hollywood, 1973

16 SERVINGS

PREP TIME: *15 minutes*

START TO FINISH: *3 hours 40 minutes*

1 cup coconut

1 cup quick-cooking or old-fashioned oats

³/₄ cup packed brown sugar

¹/₂ cup all-purpose flour

¹/₂ cup chopped pecans

¹/₂ cup butter or margarine

1 ¹/₂ cups sliced very ripe bananas (2 large)

¹/₂ cup sour cream

4 eggs

1 box (18.25 oz) yellow cake mix with pudding

1 Heat oven to 350°F. Grease 10-inch tube cake pan with shortening; lightly flour. In medium bowl, mix coconut, oats, brown sugar, flour and pecans. With fork or pastry blender, cut in butter until mixture is crumbly; set aside.

2 In large bowl, beat bananas, sour cream and eggs with electric mixer on medium speed until smooth. Add cake mix; beat on high speed 2 minutes.

3 Spread ¹/₃ of batter in pan; sprinkle with ¹/₃ of coconut mixture. Repeat layers 2 more times using remaining batter and coconut mixture, ending with coconut mixture.

4 Bake 50 to 60 minutes or until toothpick inserted near center comes out clean. Cool upright in pan 15 minutes. Remove from pan; place on serving plate, coconut side up. Cool completely, about 2 hours, before serving.

High Altitude (3500–6500 ft): Decrease butter to 6 tablespoons. Bake 60 to 65 minutes.

1 Serving: Calories 360 (Calories from Fat 140); Total Fat 16g (Saturated Fat 8g, Trans Fat 1g); Cholesterol 75mg; Sodium 290mg; Total Carbohydrate 50g (Dietary Fiber 2g, Sugars 29g); Protein 4g **% Daily Value:** Vitamin A 6%; Vitamin C 0%; Calcium 8%; Iron 8% **Exchanges:** 1 Starch, 2 Other Carbohydrate, 3 Fat **Carbohydrate Choices:** 3

kentucky butter cake

ALBERT G. LEWIS, JR.

Platte City, MO

Bake-Off® Contest 15 • Los Angeles, 1963

12 SERVINGS

PREP TIME: *30 minutes*

START TO FINISH: *3 hours 20 minutes*

CAKE

2 cups granulated sugar

1 cup butter or margarine, softened

2 teaspoons vanilla or rum extract

4 eggs

3 cups all-purpose flour

1 teaspoon salt

1 teaspoon baking powder

$^1/_2$ teaspoon baking soda

1 cup buttermilk*

BUTTER SAUCE

$^3/_4$ cup granulated sugar

$^1/_3$ cup butter

3 tablespoons water

1 to 2 teaspoons vanilla or rum extract

GARNISH

2 to 3 teaspoons powdered sugar

1 Heat oven to 325°F. Generously grease 12-cup fluted tube cake pan or 10-inch tube cake pan with shortening; lightly flour. In large bowl, beat 2 cups granulated sugar and 1 cup butter with electric mixer on medium speed until well blended. Beat in 2 teaspoons vanilla and eggs. Add flour and all remaining cake ingredients; beat on low speed until moistened. Beat on medium speed 3 minutes. Pour batter into pan.

2 Bake 55 to 70 minutes or until toothpick inserted in center comes out clean.

3 In 1-quart saucepan, cook all sauce ingredients over low heat, stirring occasionally, until butter melts. DO NOT BOIL. With long-tined fork, pierce cake 10 to 12 times. Slowly pour hot sauce over warm cake. Let stand until sauce is absorbed, 5 to 10 minutes.

4 Invert cake onto serving plate. Cool completely, about 1 hour 30 minutes. Just before serving, sprinkle with powdered sugar.

High Altitude (3500–6500 ft): Heat oven to 350°F.

To substitute for buttermilk, use 1 tablespoon vinegar or lemon juice plus milk to make 1 cup.

1 Serving: Calories 520 (Calories from Fat 210); Total Fat 23g (Saturated Fat 14g; Trans Fat 1g); Cholesterol 125mg; Sodium 470mg; Total Carbohydrate 72g (Dietary Fiber 0g; Sugars 48g); Protein 6g **% Daily Value:** Vitamin A 15%; Vitamin C 0%; Calcium 8%; Iron 10% **Exchanges:** 2 Starch, 3 Other Carbohydrate, 4 Fat **Carbohydrate Choices:** 5

butterscotch-rum ripple cake

16 SERVINGS

PREP TIME: *30 minutes*

START TO FINISH: *3 hours 15 minutes*

CLARANNE M. SCHIRLE

San Jose, CA

Bake-Off® Contest 23 • Houston, 1972

1 Heat oven to 325°F (300°F for pan with colored outer surface). Grease 12-cup fluted tube cake pan or 10-inch tube cake pan with shortening; lightly flour (if fluted pan has opening in center tube, cover with foil).

2 In large bowl, beat all cake ingredients with electric mixer on medium speed 3 minutes. Place 2 cups batter in small bowl; beat in all ripple ingredients on medium speed 1 minute. Spoon half of cake batter into pan, then half of ripple batter. Marble layers with knife in a folding motion, turning pan while folding. Repeat with remaining batters; marble with knife.

3 Bake 1 hour 20 minutes to 1 hour 30 minutes or until toothpick inserted near center comes out clean. Cool cake upright in pan 15 minutes. Place heatproof serving plate upside down over pan; turn plate and pan over. Remove pan. Cool completely, about 1 hour.

4 In 1-quart saucepan, heat $^1/_4$ cup butter and the brown sugar over medium-high heat to boiling, stirring constantly, until thickened. Remove from heat. Stir in powdered sugar and 1 teaspoon rum extract. Stir in enough water until drizzling consistency. Drizzle glaze over cake. Sprinkle with nuts. Serve warm or cool.

High Altitude (3500–6500 ft): Heat oven to 350°F. Decrease butterscotch topping to $^1/_2$ cup. Bake 1 hour 10 minutes to 1 hour 15 minutes.

CAKE

3 cups all-purpose flour

2 cups granulated sugar

1 teaspoon baking soda

1 teaspoon salt

1 cup butter or margarine, softened

1 cup sour cream

1 tablespoon rum extract

1 teaspoon vanilla

5 eggs (1 cup)

RIPPLE

1 box (4-serving size) butterscotch instant pudding and pie filling mix

$^3/_4$ cup butterscotch topping (from 12.25-oz jar)

1 egg

GLAZE AND GARNISH

$^1/_4$ cup butter or margarine

$^1/_4$ cup packed brown sugar

1 cup powdered sugar

1 teaspoon rum extract

1 to 3 tablespoons hot water

2 tablespoons chopped nuts

1 Serving: Calories 490 (Calories from Fat 180); Total Fat 20g (Saturated Fat 12g; Trans Fat 1g); Cholesterol 125mg; Sodium 500mg; Total Carbohydrate 71g (Dietary Fiber 0g; Sugars 49g); Protein 6g **% Daily Value:** Vitamin A 15%; Vitamin C 0%; Calcium 4%; Iron 8% **Exchanges:** 1 $^1/_2$ Starch, 3 Other Carbohydrate, 4 Fat **Carbohydrate Choices:** 5

caramel in-between fudge cake

JUDEE DISCO

Norwich, CT

Bake-Off® Contest 21 • San Diego, 1970

18 SERVINGS

PREP TIME: *35 minutes*

START TO FINISH: *2 hours 30 minutes*

FILLING

28 caramels (half of 14-oz bag), unwrapped

1 tablespoon butter or margarine

1 can (14 oz) sweetened condensed milk (not evaporated)

CAKE

1 box (19.5 oz) dark chocolate cake mix with pudding

1 cup water

1 tablespoon shortening, if desired

3 eggs

FROSTING AND GARNISH

$1/2$ cup butter or margarine, softened

2 envelopes (1 oz each) premelted unsweetened baking chocolate or 2 oz unsweetened baking chocolate, melted

3 tablespoons half-and-half or milk

1 teaspoon vanilla

2 cups powdered sugar

$1/3$ cup sliced almonds, toasted*

1 Heat oven to 350°F. Generously grease bottom only of 13 × 9-inch pan with shortening; lightly flour. In 2-quart saucepan, place all filling ingredients. Cook over medium-low heat about 8 minutes, stirring constantly, until caramels are melted.

2 In large bowl, beat all cake ingredients with electric mixer on low speed 30 seconds. Beat on medium speed 2 minutes, scraping bowl occasionally. Spread half of batter (about 2 cups) evenly in pan. Bake 20 minutes.

3 Spread filling evenly over partially baked cake; cover with remaining batter. Bake 20 to 25 minutes longer or until toothpick inserted in center comes out clean. Cool completely, about 1 hour.

4 In small bowl, beat $1/2$ cup butter, the chocolate, half-and-half and vanilla with electric mixer on medium speed until well blended. Gradually add powdered sugar, beating 2 to 3 minutes or until light and fluffy. Frost cooled cake. Sprinkle almonds over top.

High Altitude (3500–6500 ft): In step 1, cook filling about 13 minutes over medium-low heat. In step 3, bake 28 to 33 minutes.

*To toast almonds, bake uncovered in ungreased shallow pan in 350°F oven about 10 minutes, stirring occasionally, until golden brown.

1 Serving: Calories 390 (Calories from Fat 130); Total Fat 14g (Saturated Fat 8g, Trans Fat 0.5g); Cholesterol 60mg; Sodium 360mg; Total Carbohydrate 60g (Dietary Fiber 2g, Sugars 45g); Protein 6g **% Daily Value:** Vitamin A 6%; Vitamin C 0%; Calcium 10%; Iron 10% **Exchanges:** 1 Starch, 3 Other Carbohydrate, 2 $1/2$ Fat **Carbohydrate Choices:** 4

tunnel of fudge cake

ELLA RITA HELFRICH
Houston, TX
Bake-Off® Contest 17 • San Francisco, 1966

16 SERVINGS
PREP TIME: *35 minutes*
START TO FINISH: *4 hours 30 minutes*

CAKE

1 ³/₄ cups granulated sugar

1 ³/₄ cups butter or margarine, softened

6 eggs

2 cups powdered sugar

2 ¹/₄ cups all-purpose flour

³/₄ cup unsweetened baking cocoa

2 cups chopped walnuts*

GLAZE

³/₄ cup powdered sugar

¹/₄ cup unsweetened baking cocoa

4 to 6 teaspoons milk

1 Heat oven to 350°F. Grease 12-cup fluted tube cake pan or 10-inch tube cake pan; lightly flour. In large bowl, beat granulated sugar and butter with electric mixer on medium speed until light and fluffy. Add 1 egg at a time, beating well after each addition. On low speed, gradually beat in 2 cups powdered sugar until blended. With spoon, stir in flour and remaining cake ingredients until well blended. Spoon batter into pan; spread evenly.

2 Bake 45 to 50 minutes or until top is set and edge begins to pull away from side of pan.** Cool upright in pan on wire rack 1 hour 30 minutes. Invert cake onto serving plate; cool at least 2 hours.

3 In small bowl, mix all glaze ingredients, adding enough milk for desired drizzling consistency. Spoon glaze over top of cake, allowing some to run down sides. Store cake tightly covered.

High Altitude (3500–6500 ft): Increase flour to 2 ¹/₄ cups plus 3 tablespoons.

See photo on page 9

*Nuts are essential for the success of this recipe.

**Since this cake has a soft filling, an ordinary doneness test cannot be used. Accurate oven temperature and baking times are essential.

1 Serving: Calories 570 (Calories from Fat 290); Total Fat 33g (Saturated Fat 15g; Trans Fat 1g); Cholesterol 135mg; Sodium 170mg; Total Carbohydrate 61g (Dietary Fiber 3g; Sugars 43g); Protein 8g **% Daily Value:** Vitamin A 15%; Vitamin C 0%; Calcium 4%; Iron 10% **Exchanges:** 2 Starch, 2 Other Carbohydrate, 6 Fat **Carbohydrate Choices:** 4

chocolate praline layer cake

JULIE BENGTSON
Bemidji, MN

16 SERVINGS

PREP TIME: *25 minutes*

START TO FINISH: *2 hours 15 minutes*

Bake-Off® Contest 33 • San Diego, 1988

1 Heat oven to 325°F. In 1-quart heavy saucepan, cook butter, $^1/_4$ cup whipping cream and brown sugar over low heat just until butter is melted, stirring occasionally. Pour into 2 (9- or 8-inch) round cake pans.* Sprinkle evenly with chopped pecans.

2 In large bowl, beat cake mix, water, oil and eggs with electric mixer on low speed until moistened; beat 2 minutes at high speed. Carefully spoon batter over pecan mixture.

3 Bake 35 to 45 minutes or until cake springs back when touched lightly in center. Cool 5 minutes; remove from pans. Cool completely, about 1 hour.

4 In small bowl, beat 1 $^3/_4$ cups whipping cream until soft peaks form. Add powdered sugar and vanilla; beat on high speed until stiff peaks form.

5 To assemble cake, place 1 cake layer on serving plate, praline side up. Spread with half of whipped cream. Top with second cake layer, praline side up; spread top with remaining whipped cream. Garnish with pecans halves and chocolate curls. Store cake in refrigerator.

High Altitude (3500–6500 ft): Add $^1/_3$ cup all-purpose flour to dry cake mix; increase water to 1 $^1/_3$ cups. Bake 30 to 35 minutes and immediately remove from pans.

CAKE

$^1/_2$ cup butter or margarine

$^1/_4$ cup whipping cream

1 cup packed brown sugar

$^3/_4$ cup coarsely chopped pecans

1 box (18.25 oz) devil's food cake mix with pudding

1 $^1/_4$ cups water

$^1/_3$ cup oil

3 eggs

TOPPING

1 $^3/_4$ cups whipping cream

$^1/_4$ cup powdered sugar

$^1/_4$ teaspoon vanilla

12 to 16 pecan halves, if desired

12 to 16 chocolate curls, if desired

Cake can be made in 13 × 9-inch pan. Bake at 325°F 50 to 60 minutes. Cool 5 minutes; invert onto serving platter and cool completely. Frost cake or pipe with whipped cream; garnish. Serve with any remaining whipped cream.

1 Serving: Calories 450 (Calories from Fat 260); Total Fat 29g (Saturated Fat 12g, Trans Fat 1g); Cholesterol 90mg; Sodium 320mg; Total Carbohydrate 43g (Dietary Fiber 1g, Sugars 32g); Protein 4g **% Daily Value:** Vitamin A 10%; Vitamin C 0%; Calcium 6%; Iron 8% **Exchanges:** 1 Starch, 2 Other Carbohydrate, 5 $^1/_2$ Fat **Carbohydrate Choices:** 3

"my inspiration" cake

LOIS KANAGO

Denver, CO

Bake-Off® Contest 05 • New York City, 1953

16 SERVINGS

PREP TIME: *20 minutes*

START TO FINISH: *2 days 30 minutes*

CAKE

1 cup chopped pecans

1 box (18.25 oz) white cake mix with pudding

1 $^1/_4$ cups water

$^1/_4$ cup vegetable oil

3 egg whites or 2 whole eggs

2 oz semisweet baking chocolate, grated

FROSTING

$^1/_2$ cup granulated sugar

2 oz unsweetened baking chocolate

$^1/_4$ cup water

$^1/_2$ cup butter or margarine, softened

1 teaspoon vanilla

2 $^1/_4$ cups powdered sugar

1 to 2 tablespoons water

1 Heat oven to 350°F. Grease 2 (8- or 9-inch) round cake pans with shortening; lightly flour. Sprinkle pecans evenly in bottom of both pans. In large bowl, beat all remaining cake ingredients except grated chocolate with electric mixer on low speed until moistened, scraping bowl occasionally. Beat on high speed 2 minutes, scraping bowl occasionally.

2 Carefully spoon $^1/_4$ of batter into each nut-lined pan; sprinkle each with grated semisweet chocolate. Spoon remaining batter over chocolate; spread carefully.

3 Bake 20 to 28 minutes or until golden brown and top springs back when touched lightly in center. Cool 15 minutes. Remove from pans; place on wire racks. Cool completely, about 1 hour.

4 In 1-quart saucepan, cook granulated sugar, unsweetened chocolate and $^1/_4$ cup water over low heat, stirring constantly, until melted and smooth. Remove from heat; cool 30 minutes.

5 In small bowl, beat butter and vanilla with electric mixer on medium speed until fluffy. Gradually beat in 2 cups of the powdered sugar until well blended. Reserve $^1/_3$ cup white frosting. To remaining frosting, add cooled chocolate mixture, remaining $^1/_4$ cup powdered sugar and enough water for desired spreading consistency.

6 To assemble cake, place 1 cake layer, nut side up, on serving plate. Spread top with about $^1/_2$ cup chocolate frosting. Top with remaining cake layer, nut side up. Frost sides and $^1/_2$ inch around top edge of cake with remaining chocolate frosting. If necessary, thin reserved white frosting with enough water for desired piping consistency; pipe around edge of nuts on top of cake.

High Altitude (3500–6500 ft): Add 3 tablespoons all-purpose flour to dry cake mix; increase water in cake to 1 $^1/_3$ cups.

1 Serving: Calories 400 (Calories from Fat 180); Total Fat 20g (Saturated Fat 7g, Trans Fat 1g); Cholesterol 15mg; Sodium 270mg; Total Carbohydrate 52g (Dietary Fiber 1g, Sugars 38g); Protein 3g **% Daily Value:** Vitamin A 4%; Vitamin C 0%; Calcium 4%; Iron 8% **Exchanges:** 1 Starch, 2 $^1/_2$ Other Carbohydrate, 4 Fat **Carbohydrate Choices:** 3 $^1/_2$

ring-of-coconut fudge cake

Whitehall, PA
Bake-Off® Contest 22 • Honolulu, 1971

PREP TIME: *30 minutes*
START TO FINISH: *4 hours*

FILLING
1 package (8 oz) cream cheese, softened
¼ cup granulated sugar
1 teaspoon vanilla
1 egg
½ cup flaked coconut
1 cup semisweet or milk chocolate chips

CAKE
2 cups granulated sugar
1 cup vegetable oil
2 eggs
3 cups all-purpose flour
¾ cup unsweetened baking cocoa
2 teaspoons baking soda
2 teaspoons baking powder
1 ½ teaspoons salt
1 cup hot brewed coffee or water
1 cup buttermilk*
1 teaspoon vanilla
½ cup chopped nuts

GLAZE
1 cup powdered sugar
3 tablespoons unsweetened baking cocoa
2 tablespoons butter or margarine
2 teaspoons vanilla
1 to 3 tablespoons hot water

To substitute for buttermilk, use 1 tablespoon vinegar or lemon juice plus milk to make 1 cup.

1 Heat oven to 350°F. Generously grease 10-inch tube cake pan or 12-cup fluted tube cake pan; lightly flour. In medium bowl, mix all filling ingredients until well blended; set aside.

2 In large bowl, beat 2 cups granulated sugar, the oil and eggs on high speed 1 minute. Add all remaining cake ingredients except nuts; beat on medium speed 3 minutes, scraping bowl occasionally. Stir in nuts. Pour ⅔ of batter evenly into pan. Carefully spoon filling over batter; top with remaining batter.

3 Bake 1 hour 10 minutes to 1 hour 15 minutes or until top springs back when touched lightly in center. Cool cake upright in pan 15 minutes. Place heatproof serving plate upside down over pan; turn plate and pan over. Remove from pan. Cool completely, about 2 hours.

4 In medium bowl, mix all glaze ingredients, adding enough hot water for desired glaze consistency. Spoon glaze over cake, allowing some to run down sides. Store cake in refrigerator.

High Altitude (3500–6500 ft): No change.

1 Serving: Calories 560 (Calories from Fat 260); Total Fat 29g (Saturated Fat 10g; Trans Fat 0g); Cholesterol 60mg; Sodium 520mg; Total Carbohydrate 66g (Dietary Fiber 4g; Sugars 42g); Protein 7g **% Daily Value:** Vitamin A 6%; Vitamin C 0%; Calcium 10%; Iron 15% **Exchanges:** 2 Starch, 2 ½ Other Carbohydrate, 5 Fat **Carbohydrate Choices:** 4 ½

Pillsbury Best of the Bake-Off® Desserts

lemon platinum cake

ELIZABETH PENNEY
San Diego, CA

Bake-Off® Contest 33 • San Diego, 1988

16 SERVINGS

PREP TIME: *55 minutes*

START TO FINISH: *3 hours 50 minutes*

1 Heat oven to 325°F. In large bowl, beat egg whites with electric mixer on high speed until foamy. Add cream of tartar and $1/2$ teaspoon salt; beat until soft peaks form. Gradually add $1/2$ cup of the sugar, beating until stiff peaks form. Set aside.

2 In small bowl, beat 7 egg yolks on medium speed until lemon colored, about 2 minutes. Gradually add remaining $1/2$ cup sugar, beating until thick and light lemon colored. Add flour, $1/3$ cup lemon juice and 2 teaspoons lemon peel; beat on low speed 1 minute.

3 With spoon, gently fold egg yolk mixture into egg white mixture. Pour batter into ungreased 10-inch tube cake pan.

4 Bake 40 to 55 minutes or until top springs back when touched lightly in center. Immediately invert cake onto funnel or narrow-necked glass bottle. Cool completely, about 1 hour 15 minutes. Remove from pan.

5 While cake is cooling, in 1-quart saucepan, mix 1 cup sugar, the cornstarch and dash salt. Gradually stir in water. Cook over medium heat until mixture boils and thickens, stirring constantly; remove from heat. In small bowl, beat 2 egg yolks; gradually blend small amount of hot mixture into egg yolks. Add egg yolk mixture to saucepan; cook over low heat 2 to 3 minutes, stirring constantly, until thickened. Remove from heat; stir in all remaining filling ingredients. Cool 1 hour. Reserve $1/2$ cup filling for topping.

6 In small bowl, beat whipping cream until slightly thickened. Add reserved $1/2$ cup filling and food color; beat until thickened, about 30 seconds. DO NOT OVERBEAT.

7 To assemble cake, slice cake horizontally to make 3 layers. Place bottom layer on serving plate; spread with half of filling (about $1/2$ cup). Place middle layer on top; spread with remaining filling. Top with third layer. Spread sides, center and top of cake with topping. Refrigerate at least 1 hour before serving. Just before serving, arrange kiwifruit slices on cake. Store cake in refrigerator.

High Altitude (3500–6500 ft): No change.

1 Serving: Calories 270 (Calories from Fat 110); Total Fat 13g (Saturated Fat 7g; Trans Fat 0g); Cholesterol 150mg; Sodium 135mg; Total Carbohydrate 35g (Dietary Fiber 0g; Sugars 26g); Protein 5g **% Daily Value:** Vitamin A 10%; Vitamin C 2%; Calcium 4%; Iron 4% **Exchanges:** 1 Starch, 1 $1/2$ Other Carbohydrate, 2 $1/2$ Fat **Carbohydrate Choices:** 2

CAKE

8 egg whites

1 teaspoon cream of tartar

$1/2$ teaspoon salt

1 cup sugar

7 egg yolks

1 cup all-purpose flour

$1/3$ cup lemon juice

2 teaspoons grated lemon peel

FILLING

1 cup sugar

$1/4$ cup cornstarch

Dash salt

1 $1/4$ cups water

2 egg yolks

3 tablespoons lemon juice

1 tablespoon butter or margarine

2 teaspoons grated lemon peel

TOPPING

2 cups whipping cream

3 to 4 drops yellow food color, if desired

2 kiwifruit, peeled, sliced and cut in half crosswise, if desired

orange kiss-me cake

LILY WUEBEL
Redwood City, CA
Bake-Off® Contest 02 • New York City, 1950

16 SERVINGS
PREP TIME: *30 minutes*
START TO FINISH: *2 hours 15 minutes*

CAKE

1 orange
1 cup raisins
$^1/_3$ cup walnuts
2 cups all-purpose flour
1 cup sugar
1 teaspoon baking soda
1 teaspoon salt
1 cup milk
$^1/_2$ cup butter or margarine, softened, or shortening
2 eggs

TOPPING

Reserved $^1/_3$ cup orange juice
$^1/_3$ cup sugar
1 teaspoon ground cinnamon
$^1/_4$ cup finely chopped walnuts

1 Heat oven to 350°F. Grease 13 × 9-inch pan with shortening; lightly flour. Squeeze orange, reserving $^1/_3$ cup juice for topping; remove seeds. In blender container, food processor bowl with metal blade or food mill, grind together orange peel and pulp, raisins and $^1/_3$ cup walnuts; set aside.

2 In large bowl, beat flour and all remaining cake ingredients with electric mixer on low speed until moistened; beat on medium speed 3 minutes. Stir in orange-raisin mixture. Pour batter into pan.

3 Bake 35 to 45 minutes or until toothpick inserted in center comes out clean. Drizzle reserved $^1/_3$ cup orange juice over warm cake in pan.

4 In small bowl, mix $^1/_3$ cup sugar and cinnamon. Stir in $^1/_4$ cup walnuts; sprinkle over cake. Cool completely, about 1 hour.

High Altitude (3500–6500 ft): Heat oven to 375°F. Increase flour to 2 cups plus 2 tablespoons. Bake 35 to 40 minutes.

1 Serving: Calories 260 (Calories from Fat 90); Total Fat 10g (Saturated Fat 4.5g; Trans Fat 0g); Cholesterol 45mg; Sodium 280mg; Total Carbohydrate 39g (Dietary Fiber 1g; Sugars 24g); Protein 4g **% Daily Value:** Vitamin A 6%; Vitamin C 6%; Calcium 4%; Iron 6% **Exchanges:** 1 Starch, 1 $^1/_2$ Other Carbohydrate, 2 Fat **Carbohydrate Choices:** 2 $^1/_2$

starlight double-delight cake

HELEN WESTON

La Jolla, CA

Bake-Off® Contest 03 • New York City, 1951

12 SERVINGS

PREP TIME: *25 minutes*

START TO FINISH: *2 hours 10 minutes*

FROSTING

2 packages (3 oz each) cream cheese, softened

$^1/_2$ cup butter or margarine, softened

$^1/_2$ teaspoon vanilla

$^1/_2$ teaspoon peppermint extract

6 cups powdered sugar

$^1/_4$ cup hot water

4 oz semisweet baking chocolate, melted

CAKE

$^1/_4$ cup butter or margarine, softened

3 eggs

2 cups all-purpose flour

1 $^1/_2$ teaspoons baking soda

1 teaspoon salt

$^3/_4$ cup milk

1 Heat oven to 350°F. Grease 2 (9-inch) round cake pans with shortening; lightly flour. In large bowl, beat cream cheese, $^1/_2$ cup butter, the vanilla and peppermint extract with electric mixer on medium speed until smooth. Alternately add powdered sugar and hot water, beating until smooth. Beat in chocolate until well blended.

2 In another large bowl, beat 2 cups of the frosting mixture and $^1/_4$ cup butter on medium speed until well blended. Add 1 egg at a time, beating well after each addition. On low speed, beat in flour, baking soda, salt and milk until smooth. Pour batter evenly into pans.

3 Bake 30 to 40 minutes or until toothpick inserted in center comes out clean. Cool 5 minutes; remove from pans. Cool completely, about 1 hour.

4 To assemble cake, place 1 cake layer, top side down, on serving plate; spread with about $^1/_4$ of frosting. Top with second layer, top side up; spread sides and top of cake with remaining frosting. Store cake in refrigerator.

High Altitude (3500–6500 ft): Increase flour to 2 $^1/_2$ cups; use 1 $^1/_2$ cups of frosting mixture in cake.

1 Serving: Calories 550 (Calories from Fat 190); Total Fat 21g (Saturated Fat 13g; Trans Fat 1g); Cholesterol 100mg; Sodium 500mg; Total Carbohydrate 83g (Dietary Fiber 1g; Sugars 64g); Protein 6g **% Daily Value:** Vitamin A 15%; Vitamin C 0%; Calcium 4%; Iron 8% **Exchanges:** 2 Starch, 3 $^1/_2$ Other Carbohydrate, 4 Fat **Carbohydrate Choices:** 5 $^1/_2$

buttercream pound cake

16 SERVINGS

PREP TIME: *30 minutes*
START TO FINISH: *2 hours 55 minutes*

PHYLLIS LIDERT
Fort Lauderdale, FL
Bake-Off® Contest 19 • Dallas, 1968

1 Heat oven to 350°F. In large bowl, beat butter with electric mixer on medium speed until light and fluffy. On low speed, gradually beat in 2 ½ cups powdered sugar. On medium speed, add 1 egg at a time, beating well after each addition. Beat in lemon peel and 3 tablespoons lemon juice. On low speed, gradually beat in flour and baking powder until well blended.

2 In medium bowl, mix 3 cups of the batter and poppy seed filling. Spread half of plain batter in bottom of ungreased 10-inch tube cake pan. Alternately add spoonfuls of poppy seed batter and remaining plain batter.

3 Bake 1 hour 15 minutes to 1 hour 25 minutes or until toothpick inserted near center comes out clean. Cool 15 minutes; remove from pan. Cool completely, about 1 hour.

4 In small bowl, mix glaze ingredients, adding enough lemon juice for desired drizzling consistency; drizzle over cake.

High Altitude (3500–6500 ft): Increase flour to 4 ½ cups.

CAKE

2 cups (1 lb) butter, softened (do not use margarine)
2 1/2 cups powdered sugar
6 eggs
2 teaspoons grated lemon peel
3 tablespoons lemon juice
4 cups all-purpose flour
1 tablespoon baking powder
1 can (12 ½ oz) poppy seed filling

GLAZE

1 cup powdered sugar
1 to 2 tablespoons lemon juice or milk

1 Serving: Calories 540 (Calories from Fat 250); Total Fat 28g (Saturated Fat 15g; Trans Fat 1.5g); Cholesterol 140mg; Sodium 300mg; Total Carbohydrate 65g (Dietary Fiber 3g; Sugars 36g); Protein 7g **% Daily Value:** Vitamin A 15%; Vitamin C 0%; Calcium 10%; Iron 10% **Exchanges:** 1 Starch, 3 ½ Other Carbohydrate, ½ Medium-Fat Meat, 5 Fat **Carbohydrate Choices:** 4

Cakes & Tortes

29

nutty graham picnic cake

ESTHER TOMICH

San Pedro, CA

Bake-Off® Contest 28 • New Orleans, 1978

16 SERVINGS

PREP TIME: *30 minutes*

START TO FINISH: *2 hours 45 minutes*

CAKE

2 cups all-purpose flour

1 cup finely crushed graham crackers (14 squares) or graham cracker crumbs

1 cup packed brown sugar

$1/2$ cup granulated sugar

1 teaspoon baking powder

1 teaspoon baking soda

1 teaspoon salt

$1/2$ teaspoon ground cinnamon

1 cup butter or margarine, softened

1 cup orange juice

1 tablespoon grated orange peel

3 eggs

1 cup chopped nuts

GLAZE

2 tablespoons packed brown sugar

5 teaspoons milk

1 tablespoon butter or margarine

$3/4$ cup powdered sugar

$1/4$ cup chopped nuts

1 Heat oven to 350°F. Generously grease 12-cup fluted tube cake pan or 10-inch tube cake pan; lightly flour. In large bowl, beat all cake ingredients except nuts with electric mixer on medium speed 3 minutes. With spoon, stir in 1 cup nuts. Pour batter into pan.

2 Bake 40 to 60 minutes or until toothpick inserted in center comes out clean. Cool upright in pan 15 minutes; invert onto serving plate. Cool completely, about 1 hour.

3 In 1-quart saucepan, cook 2 tablespoons brown sugar, the milk and 1 tablespoon butter over low heat, stirring constantly, just until sugar is dissolved. Remove from heat. Stir in powdered sugar until smooth. Drizzle glaze over cake; sprinkle with $1/4$ cup nuts.

High Altitude (3500–6500 ft): No change.

1 Serving: Calories 380 (Calories from Fat 180); Total Fat 20g (Saturated Fat 9g; Trans Fat 1g); Cholesterol 70mg; Sodium 390mg; Total Carbohydrate 46g (Dietary Fiber 1g; Sugars 31g); Protein 5g **% Daily Value:** Vitamin A 10%; Vitamin C 6%; Calcium 6%; Iron 8% **Exchanges:** 1 $1/2$ Starch, 1 $1/2$ Other Carbohydrate, 3 $1/2$ Fat **Carbohydrate Choices:** 3

chocolate mousse fantasy torte

16 SERVINGS

PREP TIME: *20 minutes*

START TO FINISH: *4 hours 45 minutes*

CHRISTINE VIDRA
Maumee, OH
Bake-Off® Contest 34 • Phoenix, 1990

1 Heat oven to 350°F. Grease 9- or 10-inch springform pan with shortening. In large bowl, beat all base ingredients with electric mixer on medium speed 1 minute. Spread batter in pan. Bake 36 to 42 minutes or until set. Cool in pan on wire rack 1 hour. Remove side of pan; cool completely, about 1 hour.

2 In 1-quart saucepan, cook all topping ingredients except whipping cream over low heat, stirring constantly, until mixture is smooth. Remove from heat. Cool 15 minutes, stirring occasionally. Meanwhile, in small bowl, beat whipping cream on high speed until soft peaks form.

3 Fold warm chocolate mixture into whipped cream. With pastry tube fitted with decorative tip, pipe topping mixture evenly over cooled base or spread topping over base. Drizzle $1/2$ ounce melted chocolate over topping. Refrigerate at least 1 hour or until topping is set. Before serving, let torte stand at room temperature about 30 minutes. Store torte in refrigerator.

High Altitude (3500–6500 ft): Decrease butter to $1/3$ cup.

BASE

1 box (19.5 oz) traditional fudge brownie mix

2 teaspoons instant coffee granules or crystals

$1/2$ cup butter or margarine, softened

2 tablespoons water

2 eggs

TOPPING

1 $1/2$ cups semisweet chocolate chips

1 oz unsweetened baking chocolate

1 teaspoon instant coffee granules or crystals

$1/4$ cup water

2 tablespoons butter or margarine

1 cup whipping cream

GARNISH

$1/2$ oz unsweetened baking chocolate, melted

1 Serving: Calories 360 (Calories from Fat 180); Total Fat 20g (Saturated Fat 12g; Trans Fat 1g); Cholesterol 60mg; Sodium 190mg; Total Carbohydrate 41g (Dietary Fiber 1g; Sugars 30g); Protein 3g **% Daily Value:** Vitamin A 8%; Vitamin C 0%; Calcium 6%; Iron 10% **Exchanges:** 1 Starch, 1 $1/2$ Other Carbohydrate, 4 Fat **Carbohydrate Choices:** 3

brownie ganache torte

BARBARA ESTABROOK
Rhinelander, WI
Bake-Off® Contest 41 • Hollywood, 2004

16 SERVINGS

PREP TIME: *40 minutes*
START TO FINISH: *4 hours 50 minutes*

CRUST

1 ¼ cups graham cracker crumbs

¼ cup almond toffee bits

1 tablespoon packed brown sugar

¼ cup butter or margarine, melted

CHOCOLATE LAYER

½ cup heavy whipping cream

1 tablespoon coffee-flavored liqueur or strong brewed coffee

1 cup semisweet chocolate chips

FILLING

1 box (19.5 oz) fudge toffee or traditional fudge brownie mix

6 tablespoons butter or margarine, melted

3 tablespoons water

3 egg whites

½ cup chopped slivered almonds, toasted*

TOPPING, IF DESIRED

Whipped cream

*To toast chopped almonds, bake uncovered in ungreased shallow pan in 350°F oven about 10 minutes, stirring occasionally, until golden brown. Or cook in ungreased heavy skillet over medium-low heat 5 to 7 minutes, stirring frequently until browning begins, then stirring constantly until golden brown.

1 Lightly butter bottom only of 10-inch springform pan or spray with cooking spray. In medium bowl, mix graham cracker crumbs, toffee bits, brown sugar and ¼ cup melted butter with fork until crumbs are coated. Press in bottom of pan.

2 In 1-quart saucepan, heat whipping cream over medium-low heat until hot. Stir in liqueur. With wire whisk, stir in chocolate chips until smooth. Remove from heat. Place ¼ cup chocolate mixture in small microwavable bowl; set aside for drizzle. Pour and carefully spread remaining chocolate mixture over crust. Freeze 20 minutes.

3 Meanwhile, heat oven to 325°F. In large bowl, beat brownie mix, 6 tablespoons melted butter and the water 50 strokes with spoon (mixture will be thick). In small bowl, beat egg whites with electric mixer on high speed 1 to 2 minutes or until soft peaks form. Add to brownie mixture, beat on low speed just until blended, about 30 seconds (batter will appear lumpy).

4 Remove crust from freezer. Spread batter over chocolate layer. Sprinkle almonds evenly over top.

5 Bake 45 to 60 minutes or until center is puffed and set and edges are firm (middle will be soft). DO NOT OVERBAKE. Cool on wire rack 2 hours.

6 Run knife around side of pan; remove side. Microwave reserved chocolate mixture on High 10 to 15 seconds or until desired drizzling consistency; drizzle over torte. To serve at room temperature, cool 1 hour longer, or refrigerate until serving time. Top individual servings with whipped cream.

High Altitude (3500–6500 ft): When making crust, decrease melted butter to 3 tablespoons. When making filling, add ¼ cup all-purpose flour to dry brownie mix, increase water to ¼ cup and use 2 whole eggs (mix eggs in bowl with brownie mix, melted butter and water). Heat oven to 350°F. Bake 1 hour 5 minutes to 1 hour 10 minutes.

1 Serving: Calories 360 (Calories from Fat 160); Total Fat 18g (Saturated Fat 9g; Trans Fat 1.5g); Cholesterol 30mg; Sodium 240mg; Total Carbohydrate 45g (Dietary Fiber 1g; Sugars 33g); Protein 4g **% Daily Value:** Vitamin A 6%; Vitamin C 0%; Calcium 4%; Iron 8% **Exchanges:** 1 Starch, 2 Other Carbohydrate, 3 ½ Fat **Carbohydrate Choices:** 3

key lime cream torte

JOAN WITTAN

North Potomac, MD

Bake-Off® Contest 35 • Orlando, 1992

12 SERVINGS

PREP TIME: *35 minutes*

START TO FINISH: *4 hours 35 minutes*

CAKE

1 box (18.25 oz) butter recipe yellow cake mix with pudding

2 tablespoons lime juice plus water to equal 1 cup

$1/2$ cup butter, softened

3 eggs

FILLING

1 can (14 oz) sweetened condensed milk (not evaporated)

$1/2$ cup lime juice

2 cups whipping cream

GARNISH, IF DESIRED

Lime slices

1 Heat oven to 350°F. Grease 2 (9- or 8-inch) round cake pans; lightly flour. In large bowl, beat all cake ingredients with electric mixer on low speed until moistened; beat on medium speed 2 minutes. Pour batter evenly into pans.

2 Bake 9-inch pans 30 to 40 minutes; bake 8-inch pans 35 to 45 minutes or until toothpick inserted in center comes out clean. Cool 15 minutes. Remove from pans. Cool completely, about 1 hour.

3 In small bowl, mix condensed milk and $1/2$ cup lime juice until well blended. In large bowl, beat whipping cream with electric mixer on high speed until stiff peaks form. Reserve 1 cup of the whipped cream; into remaining whipped cream, fold condensed milk mixture just until blended.

4 To assemble torte, cut each layer in half horizontally to make 4 layers. Place 1 cake layer, cut side up, on serving plate. Spread with $1/3$ of the whipped cream filling. Repeat with second and third cake layers. Top with remaining cake layer. Pipe in decorative pattern or spread reserved whipped cream over top of torte. Refrigerate at least 2 hours before serving. Garnish with lime slices. Store torte in refrigerator.

High Altitude (3500–6500 ft): Increase water to 1 $1/4$ cups.

1 Serving: Calories 490 (Calories from Fat 240); Total Fat 27g (Saturated Fat 16g, Trans Fat 1.5g); Cholesterol 130mg; Sodium 410mg; Total Carbohydrate 55g (Dietary Fiber 0g, Sugars 40g); Protein 6g **% Daily Value:** Vitamin A 15%; Vitamin C 4%; Calcium 20%; Iron 6% **Exchanges:** 1 $1/2$ Starch, 2 Other Carbohydrate, 5 Fat **Carbohydrate Choices:** 3 $1/2$

macadamia-fudge torte

KURT WAIT

Redwood City, CA

Bake-Off® Contest 37 • Dallas, 1996

12 SERVINGS

PREP TIME: *30 minutes*

START TO FINISH: *3 hours*

FILLING

1/2 cup semisweet chocolate chips

1/3 cup low-fat sweetened condensed milk (not evaporated)

CAKE

1 box (18.25 oz) devil's food cake mix with pudding

1 1/2 teaspoons ground cinnamon

1/3 cup vegetable oil

1 can (15 oz) sliced pears in light syrup, drained

3 eggs

1/3 cup chopped macadamia nuts or pecans

2 teaspoons water

SAUCE

1 jar (17 oz) butterscotch-caramel-fudge topping

1/3 cup milk

SERVE WITH, IF DESIRED

Vanilla ice cream or frozen yogurt

GARNISH, IF DESIRED

Chocolate curls

1. Heat oven to 350°F. Spray 9- or 10-inch springform pan with cooking spray. In 1-quart saucepan, cook filling ingredients over medium-low heat, stirring occasionally, until chocolate is melted.

2. In large bowl, beat cake mix, cinnamon and oil with electric mixer on low speed 30 seconds or until crumbly (mixture will be dry). In blender or food processor, place pears; cover and blend until smooth.

3. In large bowl, beat 2 1/2 cups of the cake mix mixture, the pureed pears and eggs with electric mixer on low speed until moistened; beat on medium speed 2 minutes, scraping bowl occasionally. Spread batter evenly in pan. Drop filling by spoonfuls over batter. Stir nuts and water into remaining cake mix mixture. Sprinkle over filling.

4. Bake 45 to 50 minutes or until top springs back when touched lightly in center. Cool 10 minutes. Remove side of pan. Cool completely, about 1 hour 30 minutes.

5. In 1-quart saucepan, cook sauce ingredients over medium-low heat 3 to 4 minutes, stirring occasionally, until well blended. To serve, spoon 2 tablespoons warm sauce onto each serving plate; top with wedge of torte. Serve with vanilla ice cream; garnish with chocolate curls.

High Altitude (3500–6500 ft): No change.

1 Serving: Calories 490 (Calories from Fat 170); Total Fat 19g (Saturated Fat 6g, Trans Fat 0.5g); Cholesterol 55mg; Sodium 510mg; Total Carbohydrate 74g (Dietary Fiber 4g, Sugars 52g); Protein 7g **% Daily Value:** Vitamin A 2%; Vitamin C 0%; Calcium 10%; Iron 15% **Exchanges:** 2 Starch, 3 Other Carbohydrate, 3 1/2 Fat **Carbohydrate Choices:** 5

mocha macaroon torte

12 SERVINGS

PREP TIME: *20 minutes*
START TO FINISH: *3 hours 35 minutes*

PAMELA KENNEY BASEY
Denver, CO
Bake-Off® Contest 40 • Orlando, 2002

1 Heat oven to 350°F. Cut cookie dough in half crosswise; cut each section in half lengthwise. Press dough in bottom of ungreased 10- or 9-inch springform pan. Bake 12 to 18 minutes or until light golden brown. Cool 10 minutes.

2 While crust is cooling, in medium bowl, beat cream cheese with electric mixer on medium speed until light and fluffy. Add egg; beat until smooth. On low speed, beat in coconut, $1/4$ cup sugar, the coffee and vanilla. With spoon, stir in $1/3$ cup chocolate chips. Spoon and carefully spread mixture over crust. Sprinkle with all topping ingredients.

3 Bake 30 to 45 minutes longer or until filling is set and edges are golden brown. Cool 10 minutes.

4 Run knife around side of pan to loosen; carefully remove side. Cool 1 hour. Refrigerate until chilled, 1 to 2 hours. Serve with ice cream garnished with coffee beans. Store torte in refrigerator.

High Altitude (3500–6500 ft): In step 1, bake crust 16 to 20 minutes. In step 3, bake 35 to 50 minutes.

CRUST AND FILLING

1 roll (18 oz) refrigerated chocolate chunk cookies

1 package (8 oz) cream cheese, softened

1 egg

$1/2$ cup coconut

$1/4$ cup sugar

2 tablespoons brewed coffee

1 teaspoon vanilla

$1/3$ cup semisweet chocolate chips

TOPPING

$1/4$ cup sugar

$1/4$ cup chopped pecans

1 cup semisweet chocolate chips

SERVE WITH, IF DESIRED

French vanilla ice cream or vanilla frozen yogurt

Chocolate-covered coffee beans

1 Serving: Calories 450 (Calories from Fat 240); Total Fat 26g (Saturated Fat 12g; Trans Fat 0g); Cholesterol 45mg; Sodium 200mg; Total Carbohydrate 48g (Dietary Fiber 1g; Sugars 35g); Protein 5g **% Daily Value:** Vitamin A 6%; Vitamin C 0%; Calcium 2%; Iron 10% **Exchanges:** 1 $1/2$ Starch, 1 $1/2$ Other Carbohydrate, 5 Fat **Carbohydrate Choices:** 3

tiramisu toffee torte

CHRISTIE HENSON

Conway, AR

Bake-Off® Contest 35 • Orlando, 1992

12 SERVINGS

PREP TIME: *35 minutes*

START TO FINISH: *1 hour 20 minutes*

CAKE

1 box (18.25 oz) white cake mix
  with pudding

1 cup strong brewed coffee, room
  temperature

4 egg whites

4 toffee candy bars (1.4 oz each),
  very finely chopped

FROSTING

$^2/_3$ cup sugar

$^1/_3$ cup chocolate-flavor syrup

4 oz cream cheese, softened

2 cups whipping cream

2 teaspoons vanilla

1 cup strong brewed coffee, room
  temperature

GARNISH, IF DESIRED

Chopped toffee candy bars or
  chocolate curls

1 Heat oven to 350°F. Grease 2 (9- or 8-inch) round cake pans; lightly flour. In large bowl, beat cake mix, 1 cup coffee and the egg whites with electric mixer on low speed until moistened; beat on high speed 2 minutes. Fold in chopped toffee bars. Spread batter evenly in pans.

2 Bake 9-inch pans 20 to 30 minutes; bake 8-inch pans 30 to 40 minutes or until toothpick inserted in center comes out clean. Cool 10 minutes. Remove from pans; place on wire racks. Cool completely, about 1 hour.

3 In medium bowl, beat sugar, chocolate syrup and cream cheese with electric mixer on medium speed until smooth. Add whipping cream and vanilla; beat until light and fluffy. Refrigerate until ready to use.

4 To assemble cake, slice each cake layer in half horizontally to make 4 layers. Drizzle each cut side with $^1/_4$ cup coffee. Place 1 cake layer, coffee side up, on serving plate; spread with $^3/_4$ cup frosting. Repeat with second and third cake layers. Top with remaining cake layer. Frost sides and top of cake with remaining frosting. Garnish with chopped toffee bars. Store torte in refrigerator.

High Altitude (3500–6500 ft): Do not use 8-inch pans. Bake 9-inch pans 25 to 30 minutes.

1 Serving: Calories 480 (Calories from Fat 220); Total Fat 24g (Saturated Fat 13g, Trans Fat 1.5g); Cholesterol 60mg; Sodium 400mg; Total Carbohydrate 60g (Dietary Fiber 0g, Sugars 43g); Protein 5g **% Daily Value:** Vitamin A 15%; Vitamin C 0%; Calcium 8%; Iron 6% **Exchanges:** 1 Starch, 3 Other Carbohydrate, 5 Fat **Carbohydrate Choices:** 4

tuxedo brownie torte

PATRICIA LAPIEZO
LaMesa, CA
Bake-Off® Contest 35 • Orlando, 1992

16 SERVINGS
PREP TIME: *45 minutes*
START TO FINISH: *4 hours 15 minutes*

BROWNIE
1 box (19.5 oz) traditional fudge
   brownie mix
$^1/_2$ cup vegetable oil
$^1/_4$ cup water
2 eggs

FILLING
1 package (10 oz) frozen raspberries
   in syrup, thawed
1 tablespoon granulated sugar
1 tablespoon cornstarch
1 cup fresh raspberries or frozen whole
   raspberries without syrup, thawed,
   drained on paper towel, reserving
   3 for garnish

TOPPING
1 package (8 oz) cream cheese,
   softened
$^1/_3$ cup powdered sugar
2 tablespoons white crème de cacao,
   if desired
1 cup white vanilla baking chips,
   melted
1 cup whipping cream, whipped

GARNISH
1 tablespoon grated semisweet
   baking chocolate
3 whole fresh or frozen raspberries,
   if desired
3 fresh mint leaves, if desired

1 Heat oven to 350°F. Grease bottom and side of 9- or 10-inch springform pan with shortening. In large bowl, beat all brownie ingredients 50 strokes with spoon. Spread batter in pan.

2 Bake 40 to 45 minutes or until center is set. Cool 30 minutes. Run knife around side of pan to loosen; remove side. Cool completely, about 30 minutes.

3 In blender or food processor, blend thawed raspberries in syrup until smooth. Place strainer over small bowl; pour berries into strainer. Press berries with back of spoon through strainer to remove seeds; discard seeds.

4 In 1-quart saucepan, mix granulated sugar and cornstarch. Gradually add raspberry puree, mixing well. Heat to boiling. Cook until mixture is clear, stirring constantly. Cool 5 minutes. Spread over brownie layer to within $^1/_2$ inch of edge. Arrange 1 cup fresh raspberries evenly over raspberry mixture. Refrigerate.

5 In medium bowl, beat cream cheese, powdered sugar and crème de cacao with electric mixer on medium speed until smooth. Beat in melted vanilla chips until smooth. Fold in whipped cream. Cover; refrigerate 45 minutes.

6 Stir topping mixture until smooth. Spread 1 $^1/_2$ cups of the topping over raspberries. Pipe or spoon on remaining topping. Refrigerate at least 1 hour or until firm.

7 Before serving, sprinkle grated chocolate in 1-inch border around outside edge of torte. Garnish center with whole raspberries and mint leaves. Store torte in refrigerator.

High Altitude (3500–6500 ft): Add $^1/_3$ cup all-purpose flour to dry brownie mix; increase water to $^1/_3$ cup.

1 Serving: Calories 430 (Calories from Fat 210); Total Fat 23g (Saturated Fat 11g; Trans Fat 1g); Cholesterol 60mg; Sodium 210mg; Total Carbohydrate 50g (Dietary Fiber 1g; Sugars 39g); Protein 5g **% Daily Value:** Vitamin A 8%; Vitamin C 4%; Calcium 8%; Iron 8% **Exchanges:** 1 Starch, 2 Other Carbohydrate, $^1/_2$ High-Fat Meat, 4 Fat **Carbohydrate Choices:** 3

oats 'n honey granola pie

SUZANNE CONRAD
Findlay, OH
Bake-Off® Contest 41 • Hollywood, 2004

8 SERVINGS
PREP TIME: *15 minutes*
START TO FINISH: *1 hour 35 minutes*

CRUST
1 refrigerated pie crust (from 15-oz box), softened as directed on box

FILLING
$1/2$ cup butter or margarine

$1/2$ cup packed light brown sugar

$3/4$ cup corn syrup

$1/8$ teaspoon salt

1 teaspoon vanilla

3 eggs, slightly beaten

4 oats 'n honey crunchy granola bars (2 pouches from 8.9-oz box), crushed ($3/4$ cup)*

$1/2$ cup chopped walnuts

$1/4$ cup quick-cooking or old-fashioned oats

$1/4$ cup chocolate chips

SERVE WITH, IF DESIRED
Whipped cream or ice cream

1 Heat oven to 350°F. Place pie crust in 9-inch glass pie plate as directed on box for One-Crust Filled Pie.

2 In large microwavable bowl, microwave butter uncovered on High 50 to 60 seconds or until melted. Stir in brown sugar and corn syrup until blended. Beat in salt, vanilla and eggs. Stir in remaining filling ingredients. Pour into crust-lined pie plate. Cover crust edge with 2- to 3-inch-wide strips of foil to prevent excessive browning; remove foil during last 15 minutes of baking.

3 Bake 40 to 50 minutes or until filling is set and crust is golden brown. Cool at least 30 minutes before serving. Serve warm, at room temperature or chilled with whipped cream. Store pie in refrigerator.

High Altitude (3500–6500 ft): No change.

*To easily crush granola bars, do not unwrap; use rolling pin to crush bars.

1 Serving: Calories 540 (Calories from Fat 260); Total Fat 29g (Saturated Fat 12g; Trans Fat 0.5g); Cholesterol 115mg; Sodium 340mg; Total Carbohydrate 64g (Dietary Fiber 2g; Sugars 32g); Protein 5g **% Daily Value:** Vitamin A 10%; Vitamin C 0%; Calcium 4%; Iron 6% **Exchanges:** 1 $1/2$ Starch, 3 Other Carbohydrate, 5 Fat **Carbohydrate Choices:** 4

lemon truffle pie

PATRICIA KIEWIET

LaGrange, IL

Bake-Off® Contest 35 • Orlando, 1992

10 SERVINGS

PREP TIME: *1 hour*

START TO FINISH: *3 hours*

CRUST

1 refrigerated pie crust (from 15-oz box), softened as directed on box

LEMON LAYER

1 cup sugar

2 tablespoons cornstarch

2 tablespoons all-purpose flour

1 cup water

2 egg yolks, beaten

1 tablespoon butter or margarine

$^1/_2$ teaspoon grated lemon peel

$^1/_4$ cup lemon juice

CREAM CHEESE LAYER

1 cup white vanilla baking chips or chopped white chocolate baking bar (6 oz)

1 package (8 oz) $^1/_3$-less-fat cream cheese (Neufchâtel), softened

TOPPING

$^1/_2$ cup whipping cream

1 tablespoon sliced almonds, toasted*

1 Heat oven to 450°F. Make pie crust as directed on box for One-Crust Baked Shell using 9-inch glass pie pan. Bake 9 to 11 minutes or until lightly browned. Cool completely, about 30 minutes.

2 Meanwhile, in 2-quart saucepan, mix sugar, cornstarch and flour. Gradually stir in water until smooth. Cook over medium heat, stirring constantly, until mixture boils. Reduce heat to low; cook 2 minutes, stirring constantly. Remove from heat. Stir about $^1/_4$ cup hot mixture into egg yolks until well blended. Stir egg yolk mixture into mixture in saucepan. Cook over low heat, stirring constantly, until mixture boils. Cook 2 minutes, stirring constantly. Remove from heat. Stir in butter, lemon peel and lemon juice.

3 In 1-quart saucepan, place $^1/_3$ cup hot lemon mixture; cool remaining lemon mixture 15 minutes. Into hot mixture in saucepan, stir vanilla baking chips. Cook and stir over low heat just until chips are melted.

4 In small bowl, beat cream cheese with electric mixer on medium speed until fluffy. Beat in melted vanilla chip mixture until well blended. Spread in bottom of cooled baked shell. Spoon lemon mixture evenly over cream cheese layer. Refrigerate until set, 2 to 3 hours, before serving.

5 Just before serving, in small bowl, beat whipping cream with mixer on high speed until stiff peaks form. Pipe or spoon whipped cream over pie. Garnish with toasted almonds. Store pie in refrigerator.

High Altitude (3500–6500 ft): No change.

*To toast almonds, bake uncovered in ungreased shallow pan in 350°F oven about 10 minutes, stirring occasionally, until golden brown. Or cook in ungreased heavy skillet over medium-low heat 5 to 7 minutes, stirring frequently until browning begins, then stirring constantly until golden brown.

1 Serving: Calories 420 (Calories from Fat 200); Total Fat 22g (Saturated Fat 13g; Trans Fat 0g); Cholesterol 75mg; Sodium 220mg; Total Carbohydrate 50g (Dietary Fiber 0g; Sugars 37g); Protein 5g **% Daily Value:** Vitamin A 10%; Vitamin C 0%; Calcium 8%; Iron 4% **Exchanges:** $^1/_2$ Starch, 3 Other Carbohydrate, $^1/_2$ High-Fat Meat, 3 $^1/_2$ Fat **Carbohydrate Choices:** 3

pear and currant pie

DONENE TURNER

Vandalia, MI

Bake-Off® Contest 39 • San Francisco, 2000

8 SERVINGS

PREP TIME: *15 minutes*

START TO FINISH: *2 hours 40 minutes*

1 Heat oven to 400°F. Make pie crusts as directed on box for Two-Crust Pie using 9-inch glass pie plate.

2 In large bowl, mix all filling ingredients. Spoon into crust-lined pie plate.

3 Top with second crust; seal edge and flute. Cut slits in several places in top crust. Cover crust edge with 2- to 3-inch-wide strips of foil to prevent excessive browning; remove foil during last 15 minutes of baking.

4 Bake 45 to 55 minutes or until crust is golden brown.

5 In 2-quart saucepan, mix all glaze ingredients. Heat to rolling boil. Boil 3 to 4 minutes, stirring constantly, until nuts are glazed. Carefully spoon glaze over pie. Cool at least 1 hour 30 minutes before serving. Serve pie warm or cool.

High Altitude (3500–6500 ft): No change.

CRUST

1 box (15 oz) refrigerated pie crusts, softened as directed on box

FILLING

2 cans (29 oz each) pear slices or halves, sliced, well drained

$1/3$ cup dried currants or raisins

$1/3$ cup granulated sugar

1 tablespoon cornstarch

1 teaspoon ground cinnamon

1 teaspoon fresh lemon juice

GLAZE

1 cup chopped walnuts or pecans

$1/2$ cup powdered sugar

1 teaspoon grated lemon peel, if desired

$1/4$ cup water

2 tablespoons fresh lemon juice

1 tablespoon butter or margarine

1 Serving: Calories 530 (Calories from Fat 230); Total Fat 25g (Saturated Fat 7g; Trans Fat 0g); Cholesterol 10mg; Sodium 240mg; Total Carbohydrate 73g (Dietary Fiber 5g; Sugars 39g); Protein 3g **% Daily Value:** Vitamin A 0%; Vitamin C 2%; Calcium 4%; Iron 6% **Exchanges:** 1 Starch, $1/2$ Fruit, 3 $1/2$ Other Carbohydrate, 4 $1/2$ Fat **Carbohydrate Choices:** 5

grands!® little pies

S. LEA MEAD

San Mateo, CA

Bake-Off® Contest 40 • Orlando, 2002

16 SERVINGS

PREP TIME: *20 minutes*

START TO FINISH: *55 minutes*

³/₄ cup all-purpose flour

¹/₂ cup packed brown sugar

1 teaspoon ground cinnamon

¹/₂ cup butter or margarine

¹/₂ cup chopped nuts, if desired

1 can (16.3 oz) large refrigerated original or buttermilk flaky biscuits

1 can (21 oz) apple, blueberry or cherry pie filling

1 to 1 ¹/₂ cups whipping cream

Cinnamon-sugar

1 Heat oven to 350°F. In medium bowl, mix flour, brown sugar and cinnamon. With pastry blender or fork, cut in butter until mixture resembles coarse crumbs. Stir in nuts.

2 Separate dough into 8 biscuits. Split each biscuit in half to make 16 rounds. With floured fingers, flatten each to form 4-inch round. Press each biscuit round in ungreased 2 ³/₄ × 1 ¹/₄-inch muffin cup.

3 Spoon 2 tablespoons pie filling into each biscuit-lined cup. Sprinkle each with about 2 tablespoons flour mixture. (Cups will be full.)

4 Bake 15 to 22 minutes or until golden brown. Cool 5 minutes. Remove from muffin cups; place on wire rack. Cool 10 minutes.

5 In small bowl, beat whipping cream with electric mixer on high speed until stiff peaks form. Top each serving with whipped cream; sprinkle with cinnamon-sugar. Store pies in refrigerator.

High Altitude (3500–6500 ft): Bake 17 to 22 minutes.

1 Serving: Calories 280 (Calories from Fat 130); Total Fat 14g (Saturated Fat 8g; Trans Fat 2g); Cholesterol 30mg; Sodium 340mg; Total Carbohydrate 34g (Dietary Fiber 0g; Sugars 18g); Protein 3g **% Daily Value:** Vitamin A 6%; Vitamin C 0%; Calcium 4%; Iron 8% **Exchanges:** 1 Starch, 1 ¹/₂ Other Carbohydrate, 2 ¹/₂ Fat **Carbohydrate Choices:** 2

cream cheese–brownie pie

ROBERTA SONEFELD

Hopkins, SC

Bake-Off® Contest 39 • San Francisco, 2000

8 SERVINGS

PREP TIME: *15 minutes*

START TO FINISH: *4 hours 5 minutes*

1 Heat oven to 350°F. Place pie crust in 9-inch glass pie plate as directed on box for One-Crust Filled Pie.

2 In medium bowl, beat all cream cheese layer ingredients with electric mixer on medium speed until smooth; set aside.

3 Reserve hot fudge packet from brownie mix for topping. In large bowl, place brownie mix and remaining brownie layer ingredients except pecans; beat 50 strokes with spoon.

4 Spread $^1/_2$ cup brownie mixture in bottom of crust-lined pie plate. Spoon and carefully spread cream cheese mixture over brownie layer. Top with remaining brownie mixture; spread evenly. Sprinkle with pecans. Cover crust edge with 2- to 3-inch-wide strips of foil to prevent excessive browning; remove foil during last 15 minutes of baking.

5 Bake 40 to 50 minutes or until center is puffed and crust is golden brown (pie may have cracks on surface).

6 In small microwavable bowl, microwave hot fudge from packet on High 30 seconds. Stir in 1 tablespoon water. Drizzle topping over pie. Cool completely, about 3 hours, before serving. Store pie in refrigerator.

High Altitude (3500–6500 ft): Add 3 tablespoons all-purpose flour to dry brownie mix.

CRUST

1 refrigerated pie crust (from 15-oz box), softened as directed on box

CREAM CHEESE LAYER

1 package (8 oz) cream cheese, softened

3 tablespoons sugar

1 teaspoon vanilla

1 egg

BROWNIE LAYER

1 box (15.1 oz) hot fudge swirl premium brownie mix

$^1/_4$ cup vegetable oil

1 tablespoon water

2 eggs

$^1/_2$ cup chopped pecans

TOPPING

Reserved hot fudge from brownie mix

1 tablespoon water

1 Serving: Calories 600 (Calories from Fat 330); Total Fat 36g (Saturated Fat 13g; Trans Fat 1g); Cholesterol 115mg; Sodium 350mg; Total Carbohydrate 61g (Dietary Fiber 3g; Sugars 36g); Protein 7g **% Daily Value:** Vitamin A 10%; Vitamin C 0%; Calcium 4%; Iron 10% **Exchanges:** 1 Starch, 3 Other Carbohydrate, $^1/_2$ High-Fat Meat, 6 $^1/_2$ Fat **Carbohydrate Choices:** 4

rosy raspberry-pear pie

LOLA NEBEL

Cambridge, MN

Bake-Off® Contest 39 • San Francisco, 2000

8 SERVINGS

PREP TIME: *15 minutes*

START TO FINISH: *4 hours 5 minutes*

1 box (15 oz) refrigerated pie crusts, softened as directed on box

3 firm ripe pears, peeled, cut into $1/2$-inch slices

1 tablespoon lemon juice

$1/2$ teaspoon almond extract

$3/4$ cup sugar

3 tablespoons all-purpose flour

1 cup fresh raspberries, or frozen whole raspberries without syrup, partially thawed

1 tablespoon butter or margarine, melted

1 tablespoon sugar

Vanilla ice cream, if desired

1 Heat oven to 400°F. Place 1 pie crust in 9-inch glass pie plate as directed on box for One-Crust Filled Pie.

2 In large bowl, gently mix pears, lemon juice and almond extract. Stir in $3/4$ cup sugar and the flour. Spoon about half of pear mixture into crust-lined pan. Top with raspberries. Spoon remaining pear mixture over raspberries.

3 Remove second pie crust from pouch; unroll on cutting board. With floured $2 1/2$-inch round cutter, cut 9 rounds from crust. Brush each with melted butter. Place 8 rounds, butter side up, in circle on outer edge of fruit, overlapping as necessary. Place 1 round in center. Sprinkle rounds with 1 tablespoon sugar. Cover crust edge with 2- to 3-inch-wide strips of foil to prevent excessive browning; remove foil during last 15 minutes of baking.

4 Bake 40 to 50 minutes or until crust is golden brown and filling is bubbly. Cool completely, about 3 hours, before serving. Serve pie with ice cream.

High Altitude (3500–6500 ft): Bake 45 to 50 minutes.

1 Serving: Calories 370 (Calories from Fat 130); Total Fat 15g (Saturated Fat 6g; Trans Fat 0g); Cholesterol 10mg; Sodium 220mg; Total Carbohydrate 59g (Dietary Fiber 3g; Sugars 27g); Protein 0g **% Daily Value:** Vitamin A 0%; Vitamin C 6%; Calcium 0%; Iron 0% **Exchanges:** $1/2$ Fruit, $3 1/2$ Other Carbohydrate, 3 Fat **Carbohydrate Choices:** 4

peanut butter luster pie

HELEN MACINKOWICZ
Sterling Heights, MI
Bake-Off® Contest 34 • Phoenix, 1990

12 SERVINGS

PREP TIME: *50 minutes*
START TO FINISH: *3 hours 20 minutes*

CRUST
1 refrigerated pie crust (from 15-oz box), softened as directed on box

CHOCOLATE LAYER
$1/2$ cup semisweet chocolate chips

1 tablespoon butter or margarine

2 to 3 teaspoons water

$1/4$ cup powdered sugar

FILLING
1 cup butter or margarine

1 cup packed brown sugar

1 cup peanut butter

1 container (12 oz) frozen whipped topping, thawed

TOPPING
$1/2$ cup semisweet chocolate chips

1 tablespoon butter or margarine

2 to 3 teaspoons milk

1 $1/2$ teaspoons corn syrup

GARNISH
1 cup frozen (thawed) whipped topping

2 tablespoons chopped peanuts

1 Heat oven to 450°F. Make pie crust as directed on box for One-Crust Baked Shell using 9-inch glass pie plate. Bake 9 to 11 minutes or until lightly browned. Cool completely, about 30 minutes.

2 In 1-quart saucepan, melt $1/2$ cup chocolate chips and 1 tablespoon butter with 2 teaspoons water over low heat, stirring constantly, until smooth. Stir in powdered sugar until smooth. If necessary, add additional water for desired spreading consistency. Spread mixture in bottom and up side of cooled baked shell. Refrigerate.

3 In 2-quart saucepan, cook 1 cup butter and the brown sugar over medium heat, stirring frequently, until butter is melted and mixture is smooth. Refrigerate 10 minutes.

4 In large bowl, beat peanut butter and brown sugar mixture with electric mixer on low speed until blended. Beat on medium-high speed 1 minute. Add container of whipped topping; beat on low speed 1 minute longer or until filling is smooth and creamy. Pour over chocolate layer. Refrigerate.

5 In 1-quart saucepan, melt $1/2$ cup chocolate chips and 1 tablespoon butter with 2 teaspoons milk and the corn syrup over low heat, stirring constantly, until smooth. If necessary, add additional milk for desired spreading consistency. Spoon and gently spread topping evenly over filling. Refrigerate at least 2 hours to set topping.* Garnish pie with whipped topping and peanuts. Store pie in refrigerator.

High Altitude (3500–6500 ft): No change.

*For ease in serving, use sharp knife to score chocolate topping into serving pieces before topping is completely set. To serve, use sharp knife dipped in warm water to cut through scored lines.

1 Serving: Calories 640 (Calories from Fat 400); Total Fat 45g (Saturated Fat 23g; Trans Fat 1g); Cholesterol 50mg; Sodium 330mg; Total Carbohydrate 52g (Dietary Fiber 3g; Sugars 35g); Protein 7g **% Daily Value:** Vitamin A 10%; Vitamin C 0%; Calcium 4%; Iron 6% **Exchanges:** $1/2$ Starch, 3 Other Carbohydrate, $1/2$ High-Fat Meat, 8 Fat **Carbohydrate Choices:** 3 $1/2$

raspberry-chocolate truffle pie

12 SERVINGS

PREP TIME: *40 minutes*

START TO FINISH: *2 hours 10 minutes*

CAROL HIRD

Madison, WI

Bake-Off® Contest 33 • San Diego, 1988

1 Heat oven to 450°F. Make pie crust as directed on box for One-Crust Baked Shell using 9-inch glass pie plate. Bake 9 to 11 minutes or until lightly browned. Cool completely, about 30 minutes.

2 Meanwhile, to prepare sauce, press 4 cups raspberries through strainer to make 1 cup puree; discard seeds. In 1-quart saucepan, mix granulated sugar and cream of tartar. Stir in puree. Heat to boiling over medium heat. Boil 3 minutes, stirring constantly. Cover; refrigerate until serving time.

3 In 2-quart heavy saucepan, mix condensed milk and $^2/_3$ cup whipping cream. Heat to boiling over medium heat, stirring occasionally. Remove from heat; cool 5 minutes.

4 In food processor, process milk mixture and melted chocolates 5 to 10 seconds.* Add egg yolks; process 5 seconds. Add raspberry-flavored liqueur and amaretto; process 5 seconds longer. Pour filling into large bowl; set over ice. Stir 5 to 7 minutes or until filling is cool.

5 With electric mixer, beat cooled filling on high speed 2 to 3 minutes or until soft peaks form. Pour into cooled baked shell. Refrigerate until firm, about 1 hour, before serving.

6 Just before serving, in small bowl, beat 1 $^1/_3$ cups whipping cream with mixer on high speed until soft peaks form. Beat in powdered sugar and vanilla until stiff peaks form. Spread topping over pie. Garnish with chocolate curls and whole raspberries. Serve pie with raspberry sauce. Store pie in refrigerator.

High Altitude (3500–6500 ft): No change.

Electric mixer can be used. In large bowl, beat milk mixture and melted chocolates on medium speed 30 seconds. Add egg yolks; beat 15 seconds. Add raspberry-flavored liqueur and amaretto; beat 30 seconds or until smooth.

1 Serving: Calories 480 (Calories from Fat 250); Total Fat 28g (Saturated Fat 16g; Trans Fat 0g); Cholesterol 85mg; Sodium 110mg; Total Carbohydrate 53g (Dietary Fiber 8g; Sugars 33g); Protein 5g **% Daily Value:** Vitamin A 10%; Vitamin C 20%; Calcium 10%; Iron 15% **Exchanges:** 1 $^1/_2$ Starch, 2 Other Carbohydrate, 5 Fat **Carbohydrate Choices:** 3 $^1/_2$

CRUST

1 refrigerated pie crust (from 15-oz box), softened as directed on box

SAUCE

4 cups frozen raspberries without syrup, thawed

$^3/_4$ cup granulated sugar

$^1/_4$ teaspoon cream of tartar

FILLING

$^1/_2$ cup sweetened condensed milk (not evaporated)

$^2/_3$ cup whipping cream

5 oz semisweet baking chocolate, melted

4 oz unsweetened baking chocolate, melted

2 pasteurized egg yolks

2 tablespoons raspberry-flavored liqueur**

2 tablespoons amaretto***

TOPPING

1 $^1/_3$ cups whipping cream

2 tablespoons powdered sugar

$^1/_2$ teaspoon vanilla

GARNISH, IF DESIRED

Chocolate curls

Whole raspberries

One teaspoon raspberry extract plus enough water to measure 2 tablespoons can be substituted for the raspberry-flavored liqueur.

**One teaspoon almond extract plus enough water to measure 2 tablespoons can be substituted for the amaretto.*

greek walnut pie

MARIA E. IRVINE
San Leandro, CA
Bake-Off® Contest 41 • Hollywood, 2004

12 SERVINGS

PREP TIME: *25 minutes*
START TO FINISH: *4 hours 15 minutes*

PIE

1 box (15 oz) refrigerated pie crusts, softened as directed on box

2 1/2 cups finely chopped walnuts

1/4 cup packed brown sugar

2 tablespoons granulated sugar

1 1/2 teaspoons ground cinnamon

3/4 cup butter or margarine, melted, cooled

3/4 cup honey

1 tablespoon lemon juice

TOPPING

1/2 pint (1 cup) heavy whipping cream

1 teaspoon granulated sugar

1 teaspoon vanilla

1 Heat oven to 325°F. Spray 9-inch glass pie plate with cooking spray. Make pie crusts as directed on box for Two-Crust Pie using sprayed pie plate.

2 In medium bowl, mix walnuts, brown sugar, 2 tablespoons granulated sugar and the cinnamon. Pour and evenly spread 1/4 cup of the cooled melted butter over bottom of pie crust. Spread walnut mixture evenly over butter. Drizzle another 1/4 cup butter over nut mixture.

3 Top with second crust; seal edge and flute. Cut large slits in several places in top crust. Drizzle remaining 1/4 cup butter evenly over top crust.

4 Bake 45 to 55 minutes or until golden brown. About 5 minutes before removing pie from oven, in 1-quart saucepan, cook honey and lemon juice over medium heat, stirring frequently, until mixture has a watery consistency.

5 Remove pie from oven; place on wire rack. Slowly pour hot honey mixture evenly over top of hot pie, making sure it seeps into slits in top crust. Cool at least 3 hours before serving.

6 Just before serving, in small bowl, beat topping ingredients with electric mixer on high speed about 2 minutes or until stiff peaks form. Spoon topping onto individual servings of pie.

High Altitude (3500–6500 ft): Bake 55 to 65 minutes.

1 Serving: Calories 590 (Calories from Fat 390); Total Fat 43g (Saturated Fat 16g; Trans Fat 1g); Cholesterol 60mg; Sodium 240mg; Total Carbohydrate 46g (Dietary Fiber 2g; Sugars 26g); Protein 4g **% Daily Value:** Vitamin A 10%; Vitamin C 0%; Calcium 4%; Iron 6% **Exchanges:** 1 Starch, 2 Other Carbohydrate, 8 1/2 Fat **Carbohydrate Choices:** 3

chocolate-caramel satin pie

PHELLES FRIEDENAUER
Rockford, IL
Bake-Off® Contest 33 • San Diego, 1988

10 SERVINGS
PREP TIME: *25 minutes*
START TO FINISH: *5 hours 20 minutes*

CRUST
1 refrigerated pie crust (from 15-oz box), softened as directed on box

FILLING
24 caramels (about 7 oz), unwrapped
$1/3$ cup water
$2/3$ cup packed brown sugar
$2/3$ cup sour cream
1 teaspoon vanilla
2 eggs, beaten
$1/2$ cup chopped walnuts
1 $1/2$ oz sweet baking chocolate, grated ($1/3$ cup)

TOPPING
1 cup white vanilla baking chips
$1/4$ cup milk
1 cup whipping cream

1 Heat oven to 450°F. Make pie crust as directed on box for One-Crust Baked Shell using 9-inch glass pie plate. Bake 8 to 9 minutes or until lightly browned. Cool slightly.

2 Meanwhile, in 2-quart heavy saucepan, cook caramels and water over low heat, stirring occasionally, until caramels are melted and mixture is smooth. Remove from heat. Stir in brown sugar, sour cream, vanilla, eggs and walnuts until well blended.

3 Pour filling into cooled baked shell. Reduce oven temperature to 350°F; bake pie 30 to 40 minutes longer or until edges of filling are set. Cool 15 minutes. Reserve 2 tablespoons of the grated chocolate; sprinkle remaining chocolate over pie. Refrigerate until filling is firm, about 2 hours.

4 In 1-quart heavy saucepan, cook vanilla baking chips and milk over low heat, stirring constantly, until chips are melted. Remove from heat; cool slightly. In small bowl, beat whipping cream with electric mixer on high speed until stiff peaks form. Fold in melted chip mixture. Spread over cooled filling. Sprinkle with reserved 2 tablespoons chocolate. Refrigerate pie at least 2 hours before serving. Store pie in refrigerator.

High Altitude (3500–6500 ft): Bake 40 to 50 minutes.

1 Serving: Calories 550 (Calories from Fat 280); Total Fat 31g (Saturated Fat 16g; Trans Fat 0g); Cholesterol 85mg; Sodium 230mg; Total Carbohydrate 63g (Dietary Fiber 0g; Sugars 44g); Protein 6g **% Daily Value:** Vitamin A 8%; Vitamin C 0%; Calcium 15%; Iron 4% **Exchanges:** 2 Starch, 2 Other Carbohydrate, 6 Fat **Carbohydrate Choices:** 4

chocolate silk pecan pie

10 SERVINGS

PREP TIME: *25 minutes*

START TO FINISH: *3 hours 15 minutes*

LEONARD THOMPSON

San Jose, CA

Bake-Off® Contest 32 • Orlando, 1986

1 Heat oven to 350°F. Place pie crust in 9-inch glass pie plate as directed on box for One-Crust Filled Pie.

2 In small bowl, beat eggs with electric mixer on medium speed until well blended. Add granulated sugar, corn syrup, butter and salt; beat 1 minute. Stir in pecans. Pour into crust-lined pie plate. Cover crust edge with 2- to 3-inch-wide strips of foil to prevent excessive browning; remove foil during last 15 minutes of baking.

3 Bake 40 to 55 minutes or until center of pie is puffed and golden brown. Cool 1 hour.

4 Meanwhile, in blender or food processor, place all chocolate filling ingredients. Cover; blend 1 minute or until smooth. Refrigerate until mixture is slightly thickened but not set, about 1 hour 30 minutes.

5 Gently stir chocolate filling; pour over cooled pecan filling in crust. Refrigerate at least 1 hour or until firm before serving.

6 Just before serving, in small bowl, beat whipping cream, powdered sugar and $^1/_4$ teaspoon vanilla with mixer on high speed until stiff peaks form. Spoon or pipe whipped cream over filling. Garnish with chocolate curls. Store pie in refrigerator.

High Altitude (3500–6500 ft): No change.

CRUST

1 refrigerated pie crust (from 15-oz box), softened as directed on box

PECAN FILLING

2 eggs

$^1/_3$ cup granulated sugar

$^1/_2$ cup dark corn syrup

3 tablespoons butter or margarine, melted

$^1/_8$ teaspoon salt, if desired

$^1/_2$ cup chopped pecans

CHOCOLATE FILLING

1 cup hot milk

$^1/_4$ teaspoon vanilla

1 bag (12 oz) semisweet chocolate chips (2 cups)

TOPPING

1 cup whipping cream

2 tablespoons powdered sugar

$^1/_4$ teaspoon vanilla

Chocolate curls, if desired

1 Serving: Calories 530 (Calories from Fat 290); Total Fat 32g (Saturated Fat 16g; Trans Fat 0g); Cholesterol 85mg; Sodium 170mg; Total Carbohydrate 56g (Dietary Fiber 3g; Sugars 34g); Protein 5g **% Daily Value:** Vitamin A 10%; Vitamin C 0%; Calcium 6%; Iron 8% **Exchanges:** 1 $^1/_2$ Starch, 2 Other Carbohydrate, 6 Fat **Carbohydrate Choices:** 4

almond macaroon-cherry pie

ROSE ANNE LEMON
Sierra Vista, AZ
Bake-Off® Contest 32 • Orlando, 1986

8 SERVINGS
PREP TIME: *20 minutes*
START TO FINISH: *1 hour*

CRUST

1 refrigerated pie crust (from 15-oz box), softened as directed on box

FILLING

1 can (21 oz) cherry pie filling

$1/4$ to $1/2$ teaspoon ground cinnamon

$1/8$ teaspoon salt, if desired

1 teaspoon lemon juice

TOPPING

1 cup coconut

$1/2$ cup sliced almonds

$1/4$ cup sugar

$1/8$ teaspoon salt, if desired

$1/4$ cup milk

1 tablespoon butter or margarine, melted

$1/4$ teaspoon almond extract

1 egg, beaten

1 Heat oven to 400°F. Place pie crust in 9-inch glass pie plate as directed on box for One-Crust Filled Pie.

2 In large bowl, mix all filling ingredients; spoon into crust-lined pie plate. Cover edge with 2- to 3-inch-wide strips of foil to prevent excessive browning; bake pie 20 minutes.

3 Meanwhile, in medium bowl, mix all topping ingredients.

4 Spread topping evenly over pie. Bake pie 15 to 30 minutes longer or until crust and topping are golden brown, removing foil during last 10 to 15 minutes of baking.

High Altitude (3500–6500 ft): No change.

1 Serving: Calories 340 (Calories from Fat 150); Total Fat 16g (Saturated Fat 8g; Trans Fat 0g); Cholesterol 35mg; Sodium 160mg; Total Carbohydrate 44g (Dietary Fiber 2g; Sugars 27g); Protein 3g **% Daily Value:** Vitamin A 2%; Vitamin C 4%; Calcium 4%; Iron 4% **Exchanges:** 1 Starch, 2 Other Carbohydrate, 3 Fat **Carbohydrate Choices:** 3

one-step boston cream pie

BONNIE SCHLUTER
Galesburg, IL
Bake-Off® Contest 23 • Houston, 1972

8 SERVINGS
PREP TIME: *35 minutes*
START TO FINISH: *4 hours 5 minutes*

PIE

5 eggs
$1/4$ teaspoon baking powder
1 cup granulated sugar
1 cup butter or margarine, softened
2 cups all-purpose flour
1 teaspoon vanilla
6 snack-size containers (3.5 oz each) vanilla pudding (from two 14-oz packages)*

GLAZE

1 tablespoon unsweetened baking cocoa
1 tablespoon vegetable oil
1 tablespoon corn syrup
4 teaspoons water
1 cup powdered sugar

1 Heat oven to 325°F. Grease 9- to 10-inch deep-dish glass pie plate or 9-inch round cake pan with shortening; lightly flour. Separate 2 of the eggs. In medium bowl, beat egg whites with electric mixer on medium speed until frothy. Beat in $1/8$ teaspoon of the baking powder until peaks form; set aside.

2 In large bowl, beat granulated sugar and butter with mixer on medium speed until fluffy. Add remaining 2 egg yolks and 3 eggs, one at a time, beating well after each addition. Add flour, remaining $1/8$ teaspoon baking powder and the vanilla; beat on medium speed 1 minute.

3 With spoon, fold 2 cups batter into beaten egg whites. Pour remaining batter into pie plate; spread evenly, forming small rim. Spoon pudding over batter (pudding should not touch edges). Spoon egg white batter around edge, then gently spread over pudding.

4 Bake 20 minutes. Reduce oven temperature to 300°F; bake 40 to 50 minutes or until top is evenly browned and toothpick inserted in center comes out clean. Cool on wire rack 20 minutes.

5 In 1-quart saucepan, heat cocoa, oil, syrup and water over medium-high heat, stirring constantly, until smooth. Stir in powdered sugar until well blended. Spread glaze over pie. Cool at least 2 hours before serving.

High Altitude (3500–6500 ft): Heat oven to 350°F. Use 10-inch deep-dish glass pie plate. In step 4, bake 20 minutes. Reduce oven to 325°F; bake 50 to 60 minutes.

*If desired, cook 1 box (4-serving size) vanilla pudding and pie filling mix (not instant) as directed on box; cool and use as pudding.

1 Serving: Calories 650 (Calories from Fat 280); Total Fat 31g (Saturated Fat 16g; Trans Fat 1.5g); Cholesterol 200mg; Sodium 320mg; Total Carbohydrate 83g (Dietary Fiber 1g; Sugars 54g); Protein 9g **% Daily Value:** Vitamin A 20%; Vitamin C 0%; Calcium 10%; Iron 10% **Exchanges:** $1/2$ Starch, 5 Other Carbohydrate, 1 Medium-Fat Meat, 5 Fat **Carbohydrate Choices:** 5 $1/2$

caramel candy pie

FLORENCE E. RIES

Sleepy Eye, MN

Bake-Off® Contest 04 • New York City, 1952

10 SERVINGS

PREP TIME: *40 minutes*

START TO FINISH: *5 hours 15 minutes*

1 In small bowl, sprinkle gelatin over water; let stand to soften. In 2-quart saucepan, cook caramels and milk over medium-low heat, stirring occasionally, until caramels are melted and mixture is smooth. Stir in softened gelatin. Refrigerate until slightly thickened, stirring occasionally, 45 to 60 minutes.

2 Meanwhile, heat oven to 450°F. Make pie crust as directed on box for One-Crust Baked Shell using 9-inch glass pie plate. Bake 9 to 11 minutes or until lightly browned. Cool completely, about 30 minutes.

3 In large bowl, beat whipping cream with electric mixer on high speed until stiff peaks form. Fold thickened caramel mixture into whipped cream. Pour into cooled baked shell. Refrigerate at least 4 hours or overnight before serving.

4 Meanwhile, line cookie sheet with foil. In 7-inch skillet, cook almonds and sugar over medium-low heat, stirring constantly, until sugar is melted and almonds are golden brown. Immediately spread on cookie sheet. Cool completely, then break apart.

5 Just before serving, garnish pie with caramelized almonds. Store pie in refrigerator.

High Altitude (3500–6500 ft): No change.

1 package unflavored gelatin

$1/4$ cup cold water

1 bag (14 oz) caramels, unwrapped

1 cup milk

1 refrigerated pie crust (from 15-oz box), softened as directed on box

1 $1/2$ cups whipping cream

$1/4$ cup slivered almonds

2 tablespoons sugar

1 Serving: Calories 400 (Calories from Fat 200); Total Fat 22g (Saturated Fat 12g; Trans Fat 0g); Cholesterol 45mg; Sodium 210mg; Total Carbohydrate 46g (Dietary Fiber 0g; Sugars 24g); Protein 5g **% Daily Value:** Vitamin A 8%; Vitamin C 0%; Calcium 10%; Iron 0% **Exchanges:** 1 $1/2$ Starch, 1 $1/2$ Other Carbohydrate, 4 Fat **Carbohydrate Choices:** 3

apple pie '63

JULIA SMOGOR

Cedar Rapids, IA

Bake-Off® Contest 14 • New York City, 1962

18 SERVINGS

PREP TIME: *35 minutes*

START TO FINISH: *2 hours 20 minutes*

CARAMEL SAUCE

28 caramels (half of 14-oz bag),
  unwrapped

$^1/_2$ cup half-and-half or evaporated milk

CRUST

2 $^1/_2$ cups all-purpose flour

$^1/_4$ cup sugar

1 $^1/_2$ teaspoons salt

$^1/_2$ cup butter or margarine

$^1/_4$ cup vegetable oil

$^1/_4$ cup water

1 egg, beaten

FILLING

6 cups sliced peeled apples
  (about 6 medium)

1 cup sugar

$^1/_3$ cup all-purpose flour

1 to 2 teaspoons grated lemon peel

2 tablespoons lemon juice

TOPPING

1 package (8 oz) cream cheese,
  softened

$^1/_3$ cup sugar

1 egg

$^1/_3$ cup chopped nuts

1 Heat oven to 375°F. In 1-quart saucepan, cook caramels and half-and-half over low heat, stirring occasionally, until caramels are melted. Keep warm.

2 In medium bowl, mix 2 $^1/_2$ cups flour, $^1/_4$ cup sugar and the salt. With pastry blender or fork, cut in butter until mixture resembles coarse crumbs. Stir in oil, water and egg. Press mixture evenly in bottom and up sides of ungreased 15 × 10 × 1-inch pan.

3 In large bowl, lightly mix all filling ingredients. Spoon into crust-lined pan. Drizzle warm caramel sauce over filling.

4 In small bowl, beat all topping ingredients except nuts with electric mixer on medium speed until smooth. Spoon over filling, spreading slightly. Sprinkle with nuts.

5 Bake 35 to 45 minutes or until light golden brown. Cool completely, about 1 hour. Cut into squares. Store pie in refrigerator.

High Altitude (3500–6500 ft): No change.

1 Serving: Calories 370 (Calories from Fat 150); Total Fat 17g (Saturated Fat 8g; Trans Fat 0g); Cholesterol 55mg; Sodium 320mg; Total Carbohydrate 50g (Dietary Fiber 1g; Sugars 30g); Protein 5g **% Daily Value:** Vitamin A 8%; Vitamin C 0%; Calcium 6%; Iron 6% **Exchanges:** 1 $^1/_2$ Starch, 2 Other Carbohydrate, 3 Fat **Carbohydrate Choices:** 3

lemon cloud pie

JERRY ORDIWAY

Jamesville, NY

Bake-Off® Contest 11 • Los Angeles, 1959

8 SERVINGS

PREP TIME: *45 minutes*

START TO FINISH: *6 hours 45 minutes*

CRUST

1 refrigerated pie crust (from 15-oz box), softened as directed on box

FILLING

1 cup sugar

3 tablespoons cornstarch

1 cup water

$1/3$ cup lemon juice

2 egg yolks, slightly beaten

4 oz cream cheese, cubed, softened

1 teaspoon grated lemon peel

$1/2$ cup whipping cream

TOPPING

$1/2$ cup whipping cream, whipped

1 Heat oven to 450°F. Make pie crust as directed on box for One-Crust Baked Shell using 9-inch glass pie plate. Bake 9 to 11 minutes or until lightly browned. Cool completely, about 30 minutes.

2 Meanwhile, in 2-quart saucepan, mix sugar and cornstarch. Stir in water, lemon juice and egg yolks. Cook over medium heat, stirring constantly, until mixture boils and thickens. Boil 1 minute. Add cream cheese and lemon peel, stirring until cream cheese is melted and mixture is smooth. Cool to room temperature.

3 In large bowl, beat $1/2$ cup whipping cream until soft peaks form; fold into lemon mixture. Spoon filling mixture evenly into cooled baked shell. Cover surface with plastic wrap; refrigerate at least 6 hours or overnight before serving.

4 Just before serving, spoon or pipe whipped cream over filling. Store pie in refrigerator.

High Altitude (3500–6500 ft): In step 2, boil mixture 2 to 3 minutes.

1 Serving: Calories 380 (Calories from Fat 200); Total Fat 22g (Saturated Fat 12g; Trans Fat 0g); Cholesterol 105mg; Sodium 170mg; Total Carbohydrate 43g (Dietary Fiber 0g; Sugars 26g); Protein 2g **% Daily Value:** Vitamin A 10%; Vitamin C 2%; Calcium 4%; Iron 0% **Exchanges:** 3 Other Carbohydrate, $1/2$ High-Fat Meat, 3 $1/2$ Fat **Carbohydrate Choices:** 3

french silk chocolate pie

10 SERVINGS

PREP TIME: *50 minutes*

START TO FINISH: *2 hours 50 minutes*

BETTY COOPER
Kensington, MD
Bake-Off® Contest 03 • New York City, 1951

1 Heat oven to 450°F. Make pie crust as directed on box for One-Crust Baked Shell using 9-inch glass pie pan. Bake 9 to 11 minutes or until lightly browned. Cool completely, about 30 minutes.

2 In 1-quart saucepan, melt chocolate over low heat; cool. In small bowl, beat butter with electric mixer on medium speed until fluffy. Gradually beat in sugar until light and fluffy. Beat in cooled chocolate and vanilla until well blended.

3 Add 1 egg at a time, beating with mixer on high speed 2 minutes after each addition; beat until mixture is smooth and fluffy. Spread in cooled baked shell. Refrigerate at least 2 hours before serving. Garnish pie with whipped cream and chocolate curls. Store pie in refrigerator.

High Altitude (3500–6500 ft): No change.

See photo on page 41

CRUST

1 refrigerated pie crust (from 15-oz box), softened as directed on box

FILLING

3 oz unsweetened baking chocolate, cut into pieces

1 cup butter, softened (do not use margarine)

1 cup sugar

$1/2$ teaspoon vanilla

4 pasteurized eggs or 1 cup fat-free egg product

GARNISH

$1/2$ cup sweetened whipped cream

Chocolate curls, if desired

1 Serving: Calories 460 (Calories from Fat 310); Total Fat 34g (Saturated Fat 19g; Trans Fat 1g); Cholesterol 150mg; Sodium 250mg; Total Carbohydrate 34g (Dietary Fiber 1g; Sugars 21g); Protein 4g **% Daily Value:** Vitamin A 15%; Vitamin C 0%; Calcium 4%; Iron 10% **Exchanges:** 2 Other Carbohydrate, $1/2$ Medium-Fat Meat, 6 $1/2$ Fat **Carbohydrate Choices:** 2

apple-nut lattice tart

MARY LOU WARREN

Medford, OR

Bake-Off® Contest 32 • Orlando, 1986

8 SERVINGS

PREP TIME: *30 minutes*

START TO FINISH: *3 hours 25 minutes*

CRUST

1 box (15 oz) refrigerated pie crusts, softened as directed on box

FILLING

3 to 3 1/2 cups thinly sliced, peeled apples (3 to 4 medium)

1/2 cup granulated sugar

3 tablespoons golden raisins

3 tablespoons chopped walnuts or pecans

1/2 teaspoon ground cinnamon

1/4 to 1/2 teaspoon grated lemon peel

2 teaspoons lemon juice

GLAZE

1/4 cup powdered sugar

1 to 2 teaspoons lemon juice

1 Make pie crusts as directed on box for Two-Crust Pie using 10-inch tart pan with removable bottom or 9-inch glass pie plate. Place 1 crust in pan; press in bottom and up side of pan. Trim edge if necessary.

2 Place cookie sheet on middle oven rack in oven to preheat; heat oven to 400°F. In large bowl, mix all filling ingredients to coat. Spoon into crust-lined pan.

3 Remove second crust from pouch; unroll on cutting board. With sharp knife or pizza cutter, cut crust into 1/2-inch-wide strips. Arrange strips in lattice design over filling. Trim and seal edge. Cover crust edge with 2- to 3-inch-wide strips of foil to prevent excessive browning; remove foil during last 15 minutes of baking.

4 Place tart on preheated cookie sheet in oven; bake 40 to 55 minutes or until apples are tender and crust is golden brown. Cool tart on wire rack 1 hour.

5 In small bowl, blend glaze ingredients, adding enough lemon juice for desired drizzling consistency. Drizzle glaze over slightly warm tart. Cool completely, about 1 hour. Remove side of pan before serving.

High Altitude (3500–6500 ft): No change.

1 Serving: Calories 350 (Calories from Fat 140); Total Fat 16g (Saturated Fat 5g; Trans Fat 0g); Cholesterol 5mg; Sodium 220mg; Total Carbohydrate 51g (Dietary Fiber 0g; Sugars 22g); Protein 0g **% Daily Value:** Vitamin A 0%; Vitamin C 0%; Calcium 0%; Iron 0% **Exchanges:** 1/2 Fruit, 3 Other Carbohydrate, 3 Fat **Carbohydrate Choices:** 3 1/2

tangy crescent-nut tart

12 SERVINGS

PREP TIME: *20 minutes*
START TO FINISH: *2 hours 25 minutes*

DEBI WOLF
Salem, OR
Bake-Off® Contest 32 • Orlando, 1986

1 Heat oven to 350°F. Lightly grease 10-inch tart pan with removable bottom with shortening.* Separate dough into 8 triangles; place in pan. Press in bottom and up sides to form crust, sealing perforations.

2 Bake 5 minutes. Cool on wire rack 5 minutes. Meanwhile, in large bowl, beat granulated sugar, flour, lemon peel, lemon juice, vanilla and eggs with electric mixer on medium speed 3 minutes. Stir in coconut and hazelnuts.

3 Gently press side of warm crust up side to top of pan. Pour filling into crust.

4 Bake 25 to 30 minutes longer or until filling is set and crust is golden brown. Cool completely, about 1 hour 30 minutes. Just before serving, sprinkle with powdered sugar. Store tart in refrigerator.

High Altitude (3500–6500 ft): No change.

1 can (8 oz) refrigerated crescent dinner rolls
1 cup granulated sugar
$1/4$ cup all-purpose flour
2 to 3 teaspoons grated lemon peel (1 medium)
3 to 4 tablespoons lemon juice (1 to 2 medium)
1 teaspoon vanilla
4 eggs
1 cup coconut
1 cup finely chopped hazelnuts (filberts) or walnuts
1 to 2 tablespoons powdered sugar

1 Serving: Calories 280 (Calories from Fat 130); Total Fat 14g (Saturated Fat 5g; Trans Fat 1g); Cholesterol 70mg; Sodium 190mg; Total Carbohydrate 32g (Dietary Fiber 2g; Sugars 22g); Protein 5g **% Daily Value:** Vitamin A 2%; Vitamin C 0%; Calcium 2%; Iron 8% **Exchanges:** $1/2$ Starch, 1 $1/2$ Other Carbohydrate, $1/2$ High-Fat Meat, 2 Fat **Carbohydrate Choices:** 2

A 10-inch round pizza pan can be substituted for the tart pan. Bake crust at 350°F 5 minutes; bake filled crust 20 to 25 minutes longer.

bananas foster tart

BRENDA ELSEA

Tucson, AZ

Bake-Off® Contest 38 • Orlando, 1998

10 SERVINGS

PREP TIME: *30 minutes*

START TO FINISH: *1 hour*

CRUST

1 refrigerated pie crust (from 15-oz box), softened as directed on box

FILLING

2 medium bananas, cut into ¼-inch-thick slices

4 ½ teaspoons light rum*

2 teaspoons grated orange peel

⅔ cup chopped pecans

⅔ cup packed brown sugar

¼ cup whipping cream

¼ cup butter or margarine

½ teaspoon vanilla

SERVE WITH, IF DESIRED

Vanilla ice cream

1 Heat oven to 450°F. Make pie crust as directed on box for One-Crust Baked Shell using 9-inch tart pan with removable bottom or 9-inch glass pie plate. Place crust in pan; press in bottom and up side of pan. Trim edge if necessary. Bake 9 to 11 minutes or until lightly browned. Cool 5 minutes.

2 In small bowl, gently mix bananas and rum to coat. Sprinkle orange peel evenly in bottom of baked shell. Arrange bananas in single layer over peel. Sprinkle with pecans.

3 In 2-quart heavy saucepan, mix brown sugar, whipping cream and butter. Cook and stir over medium-high heat 2 to 3 minutes or until mixture boils. Cook 2 to 4 minutes longer, stirring constantly, until mixture has thickened and is deep golden brown. Remove from heat; stir in vanilla. Spoon warm filling over bananas and pecans. Cool 30 minutes. Serve tart warm or cool with ice cream. Store tart in refrigerator.

High Altitude (3500–6500 ft): No change.

*To substitute for the rum, mix ½ teaspoon rum extract with 4 teaspoons water.

1 Serving: Calories 290 (Calories from Fat 160); Total Fat 17g (Saturated Fat 7g; Trans Fat 0g); Cholesterol 20mg; Sodium 130mg; Total Carbohydrate 31g (Dietary Fiber 1g; Sugars 18g); Protein 1g **% Daily Value:** Vitamin A 4%; Vitamin C 2%; Calcium 2%; Iron 2% **Exchanges:** 2 Other Carbohydrate, 3 ½ Fat **Carbohydrate Choices:** 2

fudge crostata with raspberry sauce

PAULA CASSIDY

Boston, MA

Bake-Off® Contest 34 • Phoenix, 1990

12 SERVINGS

PREP TIME: *50 minutes*

START TO FINISH: *3 hours 10 minutes*

1 Make pie crusts as directed on box for Two-Crust Pie using 10-inch tart pan with removable bottom or 9-inch glass pie plate. Place 1 crust in pan; press in bottom and up side of pan. Trim edge if necessary.

2 Place cookie sheet on middle oven rack in oven to preheat; heat oven to 375°F. In 1-quart saucepan, melt chocolate chips and 2 tablespoons of the butter over low heat, stirring constantly, until smooth. In medium bowl, mix remaining 6 tablespoons butter and $^2/_3$ cup sugar with wire whisk until light and fluffy. Stir in almonds, 1 egg, the egg yolk and melted chocolate until well blended. Spread mixture evenly in bottom of crust-lined pan.

3 Remove second pie crust from pouch; unroll on cutting board. With sharp knife or pizza cutter, cut crust into $^1/_2$-inch-wide strips. Arrange strips in lattice design over filling. Trim and seal edge. Cover crust edge with 2- to 3-inch-wide strips of foil to prevent excessive browning; remove foil during last 15 minutes of baking.

4 Place tart on preheated cookie sheet in oven; bake 45 to 50 minutes or until crust is golden brown. Cool completely, about 1 hour 30 minutes.

5 Meanwhile, in blender or food processor, place raspberries. Cover; blend on high speed until smooth. Place strainer over 1-quart saucepan; pour berries into strainer. Press berries with back of spoon through strainer to remove seeds; discard seeds. Stir in $^3/_4$ cup sugar and the lemon juice. Heat mixture to boiling, stirring constantly. Reduce heat to medium-low; boil 3 minutes, stirring constantly. Cool; refrigerate until serving time.

6 Just before serving, garnish crostata with whipped cream, chocolate curls and whole raspberries. Serve with raspberry sauce. Store crostata in refrigerator.

High Altitude (3500–6500 ft): No change.

CRUST

1 box (15 oz) refrigerated pie crusts, softened as directed on box

FILLING

1 cup semisweet chocolate chips

$^1/_2$ cup butter

$^2/_3$ cup sugar

1 cup ground almonds

1 egg

1 egg yolk

SAUCE

1 package (12 oz) frozen raspberries without syrup, thawed

$^3/_4$ cup sugar

1 teaspoon lemon juice

GARNISH, IF DESIRED

Sweetened whipped cream

Chocolate curls

Whole raspberries

1 Serving: Calories 470 (Calories from Fat 240); Total Fat 26g (Saturated Fat 11g; Trans Fat 0g); Cholesterol 60mg; Sodium 210mg; Total Carbohydrate 55g (Dietary Fiber 4g; Sugars 33g); Protein 3g **% Daily Value:** Vitamin A 6%; Vitamin C 6%; Calcium 4%; Iron 6% **Exchanges:** 1 Starch, 2 $^1/_2$ Other Carbohydrate, 5 Fat **Carbohydrate Choices:** 3 $^1/_2$

coconut-pineapple tart

MARY ANN LEE
Marco Island, FL
Bake-Off® Contest 38 • Orlando, 1998

12 SERVINGS
PREP TIME: *15 minutes*
START TO FINISH: *1 hour 5 minutes*

1 refrigerated pie crust (from 15-oz box), softened as directed on box

$^1/_2$ cup pineapple preserves

$^1/_2$ cup sliced almonds, toasted*

2 egg whites

$^1/_4$ cup sugar

1 cup shredded coconut

$^1/_2$ teaspoon vanilla

1 Heat oven to 400°F. Remove pie crust from pouch; unroll on ungreased cookie sheet. Fold in crust edge 1 inch to form border; flute. Spread preserves evenly over crust; sprinkle with almonds.

2 In small bowl, beat egg whites with electric mixer on high speed until slightly thickened. Gradually add sugar, beating until soft peaks form. Fold in coconut and vanilla. Spread over almonds.

3 Bake 15 to 20 minutes or until crust is light golden brown and top is lightly toasted. Cool 30 minutes. Serve warm or cool.

High Altitude (3500–6500 ft): No change.

*To toast almonds, bake uncovered in ungreased shallow pan in 350°F oven about 10 minutes, stirring occasionally, until golden brown.

1 Serving: Calories 200 (Calories from Fat 90); Total Fat 10g (Saturated Fat 4.5g; Trans Fat 0g); Cholesterol 0mg; Sodium 105mg; Total Carbohydrate 27g (Dietary Fiber 1g; Sugars 14g); Protein 2g **% Daily Value:** Vitamin A 0%; Vitamin C 0%; Calcium 0%; Iron 2% **Exchanges:** $^1/_2$ Starch, 1 Other Carbohydrate, 2 Fat **Carbohydrate Choices:** 2

tin roof fudge tart

M. ARLENE SCHLOTTER
El Cajon, CA
Bake-Off® Contest 35 • Orlando, 1992

12 SERVINGS
PREP TIME: *1 hour*
START TO FINISH: *3 hours 30 minutes***CRUST**

1 refrigerated pie crust (from 15-oz box), softened as directed on box

2 oz dark chocolate candy bar or semisweet baking chocolate, cut into pieces

1 tablespoon butter or margarine

PEANUT LAYER

20 caramels (6 oz), unwrapped

$^{1}/_{3}$ cup whipping cream

1 $^{1}/_{2}$ cups Spanish peanuts

MOUSSE LAYER

8 oz dark chocolate candy bar or semisweet baking chocolate, cut into pieces

2 tablespoons butter or margarine

1 cup whipping cream

2 teaspoons vanilla

TOPPING

5 caramels, unwrapped

3 tablespoons whipping cream

1 teaspoon butter or margarine

GARNISH, IF DESIRED

Whipped cream

Spanish peanuts

1 Heat oven to 450°F. Make pie crust as directed on box for One-Crust Baked Shell using 10-inch tart pan with removable bottom or 9-inch glass pie plate. Place crust in pan; press in bottom and up side of pan. Trim edge if necessary. Bake 9 to 11 minutes or until lightly browned. Cool completely, about 30 minutes.

2 In 1-quart heavy saucepan, melt 2 oz dark chocolate and 1 tablespoon butter over very low heat, stirring constantly, until smooth. Spread in bottom and up side of cooled baked shell. Refrigerate until chocolate is set, about 10 minutes.

3 Meanwhile, in 2-quart saucepan, melt 20 caramels with $^{1}/_{3}$ cup whipping cream over low heat, stirring frequently until mixture is smooth. Stir in 1 $^{1}/_{2}$ cups peanuts until well coated; immediately spoon into chocolate-lined crust.

4 In 1-quart heavy saucepan, melt 8 oz dark chocolate and 2 tablespoons butter over very low heat, stirring constantly until smooth. Cool slightly, about 10 minutes. In small bowl, beat 1 cup whipping cream and vanilla with electric mixer on high speed until soft peaks form. Fold $^{1}/_{3}$ of the whipped cream into chocolate mixture; fold in remaining whipped cream. Spread over peanut layer. Refrigerate until set, about 2 hours.

5 In 1-quart heavy saucepan, melt all topping ingredients over very low heat, stirring frequently, until smooth. Remove side of pan. Pipe or spoon whipped cream around edge of tart; drizzle with topping and sprinkle with peanuts. Store tart in refrigerator.

High Altitude (3500–6500 ft): No change.

1 Serving: Calories 510 (Calories from Fat 310); Total Fat 35g (Saturated Fat 16g; Trans Fat 0g); Cholesterol 45mg; Sodium 220mg; Total Carbohydrate 43g (Dietary Fiber 3g; Sugars 23g); Protein 7g **% Daily Value:** Vitamin A 8%; Vitamin C 0%; Calcium 6%; Iron 6% **Exchanges:** $^{1}/_{2}$ Starch, 2 $^{1}/_{2}$ Other Carbohydrate, $^{1}/_{2}$ High-Fat Meat, 6 Fat **Carbohydrate Choices:** 3

granola-apple mini cheesecakes

NICK DEMATTEO

Sunnyside, NY

Bake-Off® Contest 41 • Hollywood, 2004

24 MINI CHEESECAKES

PREP TIME: *25 minutes*

START TO FINISH: *2 hours 5 minutes*

1 box (8.9 oz) roasted almond crunchy granola bars (12 bars)

1/4 cup butter or margarine, melted

3 packages (8 oz each) cream cheese, softened

3/4 cup sugar

1 teaspoon vanilla

3 eggs

1 can (21 oz) apple pie filling

1 Heat oven to 350°F. Place foil baking cup in each of 24 regular-size muffin cups. Break 8 of the granola bars into pieces; place in gallon-size resealable food-storage plastic bag or food processor; seal bag and crush with rolling pin or process until fine crumbs form.

2 In medium bowl, mix crumbs and melted butter until well combined. Place scant tablespoon crumb mixture in each lined muffin cup; press in bottom of cup to form crust.

3 In large bowl, beat cream cheese and sugar with electric mixer on medium speed until creamy. Beat in vanilla and eggs until well combined. Cut or break remaining 4 granola bars into 1/2-inch pieces; stir into cream cheese mixture. Spoon scant 1/4 cup mixture over crust in each cup.

4 Bake 20 to 25 minutes or until set. Cool in pans on wire rack 15 minutes. Top each cheesecake with 1 tablespoon apple pie filling. Refrigerate until chilled, about 1 hour, before serving. Store cheesecakes in refrigerator.

High Altitude (3500–6500 ft): No change.

1 Mini Cheesecake: Calories 220 (Calories from Fat 130); Total Fat 14g (Saturated Fat 9g; Trans Fat 0.5g); Cholesterol 65mg; Sodium 135mg; Total Carbohydrate 20g (Dietary Fiber 0g; Sugars 16g); Protein 4g **% Daily Value:** Vitamin A 10%; Vitamin C 0%; Calcium 4%; Iron 4% **Exchanges:** 1 Starch, 1/2 Other Carbohydrate, 2 1/2 Fat **Carbohydrate Choices:** 1

pecan pie–ginger cheesecake

KATHY AULT

Edmond, OK

Bake-Off® Contest 40 • Orlando, 2002

12 SERVINGS

PREP TIME: *20 minutes*

START TO FINISH: *4 hours 10 minutes*

CRUST

1 refrigerated pie crust (from 15-oz box), softened as directed on box

FILLING

1 package (8 oz) cream cheese, softened

6 tablespoons granulated sugar

$1/2$ teaspoon vanilla

1 egg

$1/4$ cup finely chopped crystallized ginger

TOPPING

2 tablespoons all-purpose flour

$1/4$ cup butter, melted

$3/4$ cup packed brown sugar

1 teaspoon vanilla

2 eggs

2 cups pecan halves or pieces

1 Heat oven to 350°F. Place pie crust in 9-inch glass pie plate or 9-inch deep-dish glass pie plate as directed on box for One-Crust Filled Pie.

2 In small bowl, beat cream cheese, granulated sugar, $1/2$ teaspoon vanilla and 1 egg with electric mixer on medium speed until smooth, scraping bowl occasionally. Stir in ginger. Spoon and spread filling in crust-lined pie plate.

3 In medium bowl, mix flour and butter. Stir in brown sugar, 1 teaspoon vanilla and 2 eggs until well mixed. Stir in pecans. Carefully spoon mixture evenly over filling.

4 Bake 40 to 50 minutes or until center is set and crust is golden brown. Cool on wire rack 1 hour.

5 Refrigerate until thoroughly chilled, about 2 hours, before serving. Store cheesecake in refrigerator.

High Altitude (3500–6500 ft): No change.

1 Serving: Calories 410 (Calories from Fat 250); Total Fat 28g (Saturated Fat 10g; Trans Fat 0g); Cholesterol 85mg; Sodium 180mg; Total Carbohydrate 35g (Dietary Fiber 2g; Sugars 23g); Protein 5g **% Daily Value:** Vitamin A 10%; Vitamin C 0%; Calcium 4%; Iron 6% **Exchanges:** $1/2$ Starch, 2 Other Carbohydrate, $1/2$ High-Fat Meat, 4 $1/2$ Fat **Carbohydrate Choices:** 2

easy lemon cheesecake

16 SERVINGS

PREP TIME: *10 minutes*

START TO FINISH: *4 hours 10 minutes*

AMELIA VILLERS

Lee's Summit, MO

Bake-Off® Contest 36 • San Diego, 1994

1 Heat oven to 325°F. Lightly grease bottom only of 10- or 9-inch springform pan with shortening. In large bowl, beat cake mix and butter with electric mixer on low speed until crumbly. Reserve 1 cup crumb mixture for topping. With floured fingers, press remaining crumb mixture in bottom and 1 $^1/_2$ inches up side of pan.

2 In same bowl, beat all filling ingredients on medium speed until smooth. Pour into crust-lined pan. Sprinkle reserved crumb mixture evenly over filling.

3 Bake 1 hour to 1 hour 30 minutes or just until center is set and edge is golden brown. Cool on wire rack 30 minutes.

4 Run knife around side of pan to loosen; remove side of pan. Refrigerate at least 2 hours before serving. Store cheesecake in refrigerator.

High Altitude (3500–6500 ft): Bake 1 hour 20 minutes to 1 hour 40 minutes.

CRUST

1 box (18.25 oz) lemon or yellow cake mix with pudding

$^1/_2$ cup butter or margarine, softened

FILLING

2 packages (8 oz each) cream cheese, softened

3 eggs

1 container (8 oz) lemon yogurt

1 container (1 lb) lemon creamy ready-to-spread frosting

1 Serving: Calories 440 (Calories from Fat 220); Total Fat 24g (Saturated Fat 15g; Trans Fat 1g); Cholesterol 90mg; Sodium 370mg; Total Carbohydrate 50g (Dietary Fiber 0g; Sugars 43g); Protein 5g **% Daily Value:** Vitamin A 15%; Vitamin C 0%; Calcium 8%; Iron 6% **Exchanges:** 3 $^1/_2$ Other Carbohydrate, $^1/_2$ High-Fat Meat, 4 Fat **Carbohydrate Choices:** 3

peanut butter–chocolate creme cheesecake

MELISSA HENNINGER

Northport, AL

Bake-Off® Contest 36 • San Diego, 1994

16 SERVINGS

PREP TIME: *25 minutes*

START TO FINISH: *3 hours 25 minutes*

CRUST

1 ½ cups finely crushed creme-filled chocolate sandwich cookies (about 18)

6 tablespoons sugar

3 tablespoons unsweetened baking cocoa

¼ cup butter or margarine, melted

FILLING

3 packages (8 oz each) cream cheese, softened

1 cup creamy peanut butter

1 container (1 lb) vanilla creamy ready-to-spread frosting

1 ½ cups coarsely chopped creme-filled chocolate sandwich cookies (about 16)

TOPPING

4 packages (1.6 oz each) or 8 chocolate-covered peanut butter cups (.6 oz each), unwrapped, broken into pieces

¼ cup milk

1 ½ cups frozen (thawed) whipped topping

3 tablespoons unsweetened baking cocoa

2 tablespoons sugar

GARNISH, IF DESIRED

1 chocolate-covered peanut butter cup, cut into 6 wedges

1 creme-filled chocolate sandwich cookie, cut into 6 wedges

1 In blender, food processor or large bowl, mix all crust ingredients. Press in bottom of ungreased 9- or 10-inch springform pan; set aside.

2 In large bowl, beat cream cheese with electric mixer on medium speed until smooth and creamy. Add peanut butter; beat until light and fluffy. Fold in frosting. Pour half of batter over crust; sprinkle evenly with 1 ½ cups chopped cookies. Cover with remaining batter. Refrigerate until set, about 2 hours.

3 In small microwavable bowl, microwave broken peanut butter cups and milk on High 1 minute 30 seconds to 3 minutes, stirring once halfway through cooking.* Stir until smooth; pour over top of cheesecake. Refrigerate until set, about 1 hour.

4 In large bowl, gently mix whipped topping, 3 tablespoons cocoa and 2 tablespoons sugar until well blended. Remove side of pan. Pipe or spoon 12 circular mounds around edge of cheesecake; garnish with candy and cookie wedges. Store cheesecake in refrigerator.

High Altitude (3500–6500 ft): No change.

*To melt peanut butter cups on stove top, in 1-quart saucepan, heat peanut butter cups and milk over low heat 2 to 3 minutes, stirring frequently, until candy is melted and mixture is smooth.

See photo on page 71

1 Serving: Calories 620 (Calories from Fat 360); Total Fat 40g (Saturated Fat 20g; Trans Fat 2g); Cholesterol 55mg; Sodium 410mg; Total Carbohydrate 55g (Dietary Fiber 3g; Sugars 43g); Protein 10g **% Daily Value:** Vitamin A 15%; Vitamin C 0%; Calcium 6%; Iron 10% **Exchanges:** 1 Starch, 2 ½ Other Carbohydrate, 1 High-Fat Meat, 6 Fat **Carbohydrate Choices:** 3 ½

praline pecan cheesecake

16 SERVINGS

PREP TIME: *35 minutes*
START TO FINISH: *7 hours 40 minutes*

SUE ZAPPA
St. Paul, MN
Bake-Off® Contest 34 • Phoenix, 1990

1 Heat oven to 325°F. In large bowl, beat cake mix and butter with electric mixer on low speed until crumbly. Reserve 1 cup of crumb mixture for topping. With floured fingers, press remaining crumb mixture in bottom and $^1/_2$ inch up side of ungreased 10- or 9-inch springform pan.

2 In same large bowl, beat cream cheese, granulated sugar, flour and rum extract on medium speed until smooth. Add eggs; beat well. Stir in crushed candy bars. Pour into crust-lined pan.

3 In medium bowl, mix reserved crumb mixture, brown sugar and pecans. Sprinkle evenly over filling.

4 Bake 1 hour 10 minutes to 1 hour 25 minutes or until center is set and topping is golden brown. Drizzle caramel topping over top of cheesecake; bake 8 to 10 minutes longer or until topping is set. Cool on wire rack 30 minutes.

5 Run knife around side of pan to loosen. Cool completely, about 1 hour. Remove side of pan. Refrigerate cheesecake at least 4 hours or overnight before serving. Store cheesecake in refrigerator.

High Altitude (3500–6500 ft): No change.

CRUST

1 box (18.25 oz) butter recipe cake mix with pudding

$^1/_2$ cup butter or margarine, softened

FILLING

3 packages (8 oz each) cream cheese, softened

$^1/_3$ cup granulated sugar

3 tablespoons all-purpose flour

1 to 1 $^1/_2$ teaspoons rum extract

3 eggs

4 toffee candy bars (1.4 oz each), coarsely crushed

TOPPING

$^1/_2$ cup packed brown sugar

1 cup chopped pecans

1/3 cup caramel topping

1 Serving: Calories 530 (Calories from Fat 300); Total Fat 33g (Saturated Fat 16g; Trans Fat 1.5g); Cholesterol 105mg; Sodium 460mg; Total Carbohydrate 51g (Dietary Fiber 1g; Sugars 41g); Protein 7g **% Daily Value:** Vitamin A 20%; Vitamin C 0%; Calcium 10%; Iron 8% **Exchanges:** 1 Starch, 2 $^1/_2$ Other Carbohydrate, $^1/_2$ High-Fat Meat, 5 $^1/_2$ Fat **Carbohydrate Choices:** 3 $^1/_2$

apple-crescent cheesecake

EUGENE MAJEWSKI

Elmhurst, IL

Bake-Off® Contest 22 • Honolulu, 1971

10 SERVINGS

PREP TIME: *25 minutes*

START TO FINISH: *4 hours 50 minutes*

$^1/_3$ cup sugar

$^1/_2$ teaspoon ground cinnamon

3 cups thinly sliced, peeled cooking apples (3 medium)

3 packages (3 oz each) cream cheese, softened

$^1/_4$ cup sugar

2 tablespoons milk

$^1/_2$ teaspoon vanilla

1 egg

1 can (8 oz) refrigerated crescent dinner rolls

$^1/_2$ cup apricot preserves

1 tablespoon water

1 Heat oven to 400°F. In medium bowl, mix $^1/_3$ cup sugar and the cinnamon. Stir in apples until coated; set aside.

2 In small bowl, beat cream cheese, $^1/_4$ cup sugar, the milk, vanilla and egg with electric mixer on medium speed until smooth; set aside.

3 Unroll dough; separate into 8 triangles. In ungreased 9-inch springform pan or 9-inch round cake pan, arrange triangles; press in bottom and about 1 $^1/_2$ inches up side to make crust. Spoon cheese mixture into crust.

4 Drain any liquid from apples; arrange apples over cheese mixture. In small bowl, mix preserves and water; drizzle over apples.

5 Bake 20 minutes. Reduce oven temperature to 350°F; bake 30 to 35 minutes longer or until crust is deep golden brown and center is firm to the touch. Cool completely, about 30 minutes. Refrigerate at least 1 hour 30 minutes before serving.

High Altitude (3500–6500 ft): Bake 35 to 40 minutes.

1 Serving: Calories 290 (Calories from Fat 130); Total Fat 14g (Saturated Fat 7g; Trans Fat 1.5g); Cholesterol 50mg; Sodium 260mg; Total Carbohydrate 37g (Dietary Fiber 0g; Sugars 25g); Protein 4g **% Daily Value:** Vitamin A 8%; Vitamin C 2%; Calcium 4%; Iron 6% **Exchanges:** 1 Starch, 1 $^1/_2$ Other Carbohydrate, 2 $^1/_2$ Fat **Carbohydrate Choices:** 2 $^1/_2$

mocha swirl cheesecake

SUSAN PAJCIC

Jacksonville, FL

Bake-Off® Contest 30 • San Antonio, 1982

16 SERVINGS

PREP TIME: *25 minutes*

START TO FINISH: *3 hours 15 minutes*

1 tablespoon instant coffee granules
   or crystals

3 tablespoons milk

1 box (18.25 oz) dark chocolate cake
   mix with pudding

$^1/_3$ cup butter or margarine, melted

4 eggs

$^3/_4$ cup sugar

2 packages (8 oz each) cream cheese,
   softened

1 teaspoon vanilla

$^1/_2$ teaspoon almond extract, if desired

3 cups sour cream

3 to 4 teaspoons instant coffee
   granules or crystals

Sweetened whipped cream, if desired

1 Heat oven to 350°F. Grease 10-inch springform pan or 12 × 8-inch (2-quart) glass baking dish with shortening. Dissolve 1 tablespoon coffee in 1 tablespoon of the milk. Reserve $^3/_4$ cup cake mix for filling. Place remaining cake mix in large bowl; beat in butter, 1 of the eggs and the coffee mixture with electric mixer on low speed until soft dough forms. Press in bottom and up side of pan to within 1 inch of top edge.

2 In another large bowl, beat sugar, cream cheese, vanilla, almond extract and remaining 3 eggs with mixer on medium speed 3 minutes, scraping bowl occasionally. Beat in sour cream. Reserve 2 cups cheese mixture in medium bowl; set mixture in large bowl aside.

3 Dissolve 3 teaspoons instant coffee in remaining 2 tablespoons milk. Add coffee mixture and reserved $^3/_4$ cup cake mix to reserved 2 cups cheese mixture; beat with mixer on medium speed until well blended. Spoon over cream cheese mixture in large bowl. Marble by pulling knife through mixtures in wide curves; pour into crust.

4 Bake 1 hour to 1 hour 10 minutes or until knife inserted 1 inch from edge of cheesecake comes out clean. Cool 30 minutes. Refrigerate 1 hour. With knife, loosen edge; remove side of pan. Refrigerate at least 4 hours or overnight before serving. Serve with sweetened whipped cream. Store cheesecake in refrigerator.

High Altitude (3500–6500 ft): No change.

1 Serving: Calories 420 (Calories from Fat 230); Total Fat 26g (Saturated Fat 15g, Trans Fat 1g); Cholesterol 125mg; Sodium 430mg; Total Carbohydrate 40g (Dietary Fiber 0g, Sugars 28g); Protein 7g **% Daily Value:** Vitamin A 15%; Vitamin C 0%; Calcium 10%; Iron 8% **Exchanges:** $^1/_2$ Starch, 2 Other Carbohydrate, 1 High-Fat Meat, 3 $^1/_2$ Fat **Carbohydrate Choices:** 2 $^1/_2$

cherry-crescent cheesecake cups

8 SERVINGS

PREP TIME: *20 minutes*
START TO FINISH: *45 minutes*

GLEN OCOCK
Appleton, WI
Bake-Off® Contest 22 • Honolulu, 1971

1 Heat oven to 350°F. Grease 8 regular-size muffin cups with shortening. In medium bowl, beat cream cheese and egg with electric mixer on medium speed until smooth. Beat in powdered sugar, almonds and almond extract until well blended.

2 Separate dough into 4 rectangles; firmly press perforations to seal. Press or roll each into 8 × 4-inch rectangle. Cut each rectangle in half crosswise, forming 8 squares. Press each square in bottom of muffin cup, leaving corners of each square extended over side of cup.

3 Place about ¹/₄ cup cream cheese mixture into each dough-lined cup. Bring 4 corners of each square together in center of cup; firmly press points together to seal.

4 Bake 18 to 23 minutes or until golden brown. Immediately remove from muffin cups. In 1-quart saucepan, cook all topping ingredients over low heat, stirring occasionally, until bubbly and butter melts. Serve over warm desserts. Store desserts in refrigerator.

High Altitude (3500–6500 ft): Bake 20 to 25 minutes. Cool 5 to 10 minutes before removing from muffin cups.

CUPS

1 package (8 oz) cream cheese, softened

1 egg

1 cup powdered sugar

¹/₄ cup chopped almonds

¹/₂ to 1 teaspoon almond extract

1 can (8 oz) refrigerated crescent dinner rolls

TOPPING

1 cup cherry pie filling

1 to 2 tablespoons amaretto or cherry-flavored brandy

1 tablespoon butter or margarine

1 Serving: Calories 350 (Calories from Fat 180); Total Fat 20g (Saturated Fat 10g; Trans Fat 2g); Cholesterol 60mg; Sodium 320mg; Total Carbohydrate 37g (Dietary Fiber 1g; Sugars 25g); Protein 6g **% Daily Value:** Vitamin A 10%; Vitamin C 0%; Calcium 4%; Iron 8% **Exchanges:** 1 Starch, 1 ¹/₂ Other Carbohydrate, ¹/₂ High-Fat Meat, 3 Fat **Carbohydrate Choices:** 2 ¹/₂

royal marble cheesecake

ISAAC FEINSTEIN

Atlantic City, NJ

Bake-Off® Contest 16 • Miami, 1964

16 SERVINGS

PREP TIME: *35 minutes*

START TO FINISH: *12 hours*

CRUST

- $3/4$ cup all-purpose flour
- 2 tablespoons sugar
- Dash salt
- $1/4$ cup butter or margarine
- 1 cup semisweet chocolate chips, melted

FILLING

- 3 packages (8 oz each) cream cheese, softened
- 1 cup sugar
- $1/4$ cup all-purpose flour
- 2 teaspoons vanilla
- 6 eggs
- 1 cup sour cream

1 Heat oven to 400°F. In small bowl, mix $3/4$ cup flour, 2 tablespoons sugar and the salt. With pastry blender or fork, cut in butter until mixture resembles coarse crumbs. Stir in 2 tablespoons of the melted chocolate; reserve remaining chocolate for filling. Press crumb mixture in bottom of ungreased 9-inch springform pan.

2 Bake 10 minutes or until very light brown. Remove pan from oven. Reduce oven temperature to 325°F.

3 Meanwhile, in large bowl, beat cream cheese and 1 cup sugar with electric mixer on medium speed until light and fluffy. Beat in $1/4$ cup flour and the vanilla until well blended. On low speed, add 1 egg at a time, beating just until blended after each addition. Beat in sour cream. Place 1 $3/4$ cups filling mixture in medium bowl; stir in reserved melted chocolate.

4 Pour half of plain filling over crust. By spoonfuls, top with half of chocolate filling. Cover with remaining plain filling, then with spoonfuls of remaining chocolate filling. With table knife, swirl chocolate filling through plain filling. Place cheesecake in center of oven. Place shallow pan half full of water on bottom oven rack under cheesecake.

5 Bake at 325°F 1 hour to 1 hour 15 minutes or until set but center of cheesecake still jiggles when moved. Cool on wire rack 10 minutes. Run knife around edge of pan to loosen cheesecake. Cool at least 2 hours. Refrigerate at least 8 hours or overnight before serving. Carefully remove side of pan. Store cheesecake in refrigerator.

High Altitude (3500–6500 ft): In step 5, bake cheesecake at 325°F 1 hour 15 minutes to 1 hour 25 minutes. Remove from oven; immediately run knife around edge of pan to loosen cheesecake.

1 Serving: Calories 370 (Calories from Fat 230); Total Fat 26g (Saturated Fat 15g; Trans Fat 0.5g); Cholesterol 145mg; Sodium 190mg; Total Carbohydrate 29g (Dietary Fiber 0g; Sugars 21g); Protein 7g **% Daily Value:** Vitamin A 15%; Vitamin C 0%; Calcium 6%; Iron 8% **Exchanges:** 2 Other Carbohydrate, 1 High-Fat Meat, 3 $1/2$ Fat **Carbohydrate Choices:** 2

sher-riffic marble cheesecake

BETTY ENGLES

Midland, MI

Bake-Off® Contest 21 • San Diego, 1970

10 SERVINGS

PREP TIME: *45 minutes*

START TO FINISH: *1 hour 45 minutes*

CRUST

1 cup all-purpose flour

$^1/_2$ teaspoon salt

$^1/_2$ cup butter or margarine

1 $^1/_2$ to 2 tablespoons cold water

$^1/_2$ to 1 teaspoon lemon extract

FILLING

2 packages (8 oz each) cream cheese, softened

1 can (14 oz) sweetened condensed milk (not evaporated)

1 box (4-serving size) lemon or vanilla instant pudding and pie filling mix

$^1/_3$ cup cream sherry or milk

1 envelope (1 oz) premelted unsweetened baking chocolate or 1 oz unsweetened baking chocolate, melted

1 to 2 tablespoons cream sherry or milk

1 Heat oven to 450°F. In medium bowl, mix flour and salt. With pastry blender or fork, cut in butter until crumbly. With fork, lightly stir in water and lemon extract just until dough holds together. With floured fingers, press dough in bottom and 1 inch up side of ungreased 9-inch springform pan or 9-inch round or square cake pan. Bake 12 to 15 minutes or until light golden brown. Cool 15 minutes.

2 Meanwhile, in small bowl, beat cream cheese with electric mixer on medium speed until fluffy. On low speed, beat in $^2/_3$ cup of the condensed milk and the dry pudding mix until smooth. Gradually add $^1/_3$ cup sherry, beating until thoroughly combined, about 1 minute.

3 In 1-quart saucepan, heat remaining $^2/_3$ cup condensed milk and the chocolate over medium heat, stirring constantly, until thickened. Remove from heat. Stir in 1 to 2 tablespoons sherry until mixture is thin enough to drizzle.

4 Spread cream cheese mixture in cooled crust; drizzle with chocolate mixture. With knife, cut through both mixtures to marble slightly. Refrigerate at least 1 hour before serving. Store cheesecake in refrigerator.

High Altitude (3500–6500 ft): No change.

1 Serving: Calories 480 (Calories from Fat 270); Total Fat 30g (Saturated Fat 19g; Trans Fat 1g); Cholesterol 90mg; Sodium 510mg; Total Carbohydrate 44g (Dietary Fiber 0g; Sugars 31g); Protein 8g **% Daily Value:** Vitamin A 20%; Vitamin C 0%; Calcium 15%; Iron 10% **Exchanges:** $^1/_2$ Starch, 2 $^1/_2$ Other Carbohydrate, 1 High-Fat Meat, 4 $^1/_2$ Fat **Carbohydrate Choices:** 3

caramel-pear-pecan flan

8 SERVINGS

PREP TIME: *30 minutes*

START TO FINISH: *3 hours 30 minutes*

TILLIE ASTORINO

North Adams, MA

Bake-Off® Contest 32 • Orlando, 1986

1 Place pie crust in 10-inch microwavable tart pan or 9-inch microwavable pie plate as directed on box for One-Crust Filled Pie. Press $^1/_2$ cup pecans on bottom and side of crust. Microwave on High 6 to 8 minutes, rotating pan $^1/_2$ turn every 2 minutes. Crust is done when surface appears dry and flaky.

2 In small bowl, beat cream cheese, $^1/_2$ cup of the caramel topping and the eggs with electric mixer on medium speed until smooth and creamy. Pour into cooked crust.

3 Arrange pear slices in single layer over cream cheese mixture. For tart pan, microwave on High 6 to 9 minutes (for pie plate, 9 to 11 minutes), rotating pan $^1/_4$ turn every 3 minutes. Pie is done when center is almost set (cream cheese mixture will firm up as it cools and chills). Cover loosely with waxed paper; cool on flat surface 1 hour. Refrigerate at least 2 hours or until serving time.

4 Just before serving, top with whipped topping. Drizzle with remaining $^1/_4$ to $^1/_2$ cup caramel topping; sprinkle with 3 tablespoons pecans. Store flan in refrigerator.

High Altitude (3500–6500 ft): No change.

CRUST

1 refrigerated pie crust (from 15-oz box), softened as directed on box

$^1/_2$ cup chopped pecans

FILLING

1 package (8 oz) cream cheese, softened

$^3/_4$ to 1 cup caramel topping

2 eggs

1 can (29 oz) pear halves, well drained, sliced*

1 $^1/_2$ cups frozen (thawed) whipped topping

3 tablespoons chopped pecans

Six to 10 canned pear halves, arranged with rounded sides up and narrow ends pointing toward center, can be substituted for the sliced pears. If desired, score pears by making $^1/_8$-inch-deep decorative cuts on pear halves.

1 Serving: Calories 460 (Calories from Fat 250); Total Fat 28g (Saturated Fat 12g; Trans Fat 0g); Cholesterol 90mg; Sodium 320mg; Total Carbohydrate 47g (Dietary Fiber 3g; Sugars 25g); Protein 5g **% Daily Value:** Vitamin A 10%; Vitamin C 0%; Calcium 6%; Iron 6% **Exchanges:** 1 Starch, 2 Other Carbohydrate, 5 $^1/_2$ Fat **Carbohydrate Choices:** 3

streusel fruit custard

MARTIE A. KIAN
Edinboro, PA
Bake-Off® Contest 24 • Hollywood, 1973

6 SERVINGS
PREP TIME: *15 minutes*
START TO FINISH: *1 hour 10 minutes*

FRUIT MIXTURE

1 can (15.25 oz) sliced pears, drained

1 can (15.25 oz) sliced peaches, drained

2 eggs

¹/₄ cup all-purpose flour

¹/₄ cup sugar

1 cup sour cream

1 teaspoon vanilla

TOPPING

³/₄ cup all-purpose flour

¹/₂ cup packed brown sugar

¹/₂ teaspoon ground nutmeg

¹/₄ cup butter or margarine, softened

SERVE WITH, IF DESIRED

Vanilla ice cream or whipped cream

1 Heat oven to 325°F. In ungreased 8-inch square or 11 × 7-inch (2-quart) glass baking dish, arrange pears and peaches. In medium bowl, beat eggs with wire whisk until blended. Beat in remaining fruit mixture ingredients until smooth. Pour over fruit.

2 In same bowl, mix all topping ingredients until crumbly. Sprinkle over fruit mixture.

3 Bake 30 to 40 minutes or until topping is golden brown and center is set. Cool at least 15 minutes. Serve warm with ice cream. Store custard in refrigerator.

High Altitude (3500–6500 ft): Heat oven to 350°F. Bake 50 to 60 minutes.

1 Serving: Calories 390 (Calories from Fat 150); Total Fat 17g (Saturated Fat 10g; Trans Fat 0.5g); Cholesterol 115mg; Sodium 100mg; Total Carbohydrate 54g (Dietary Fiber 3g; Sugars 36g); Protein 6g **% Daily Value:** Vitamin A 20%; Vitamin C 2%; Calcium 8%; Iron 10% **Exchanges:** 2 Starch, 1 ¹/₂ Other Carbohydrate, 3 Fat **Carbohydrate Choices:** 3 ¹/₂

caramel apple pudding

CLIFTON G. MANDRELL
Russell, KY
Bake-Off® Contest 09 • Los Angeles, 1957

6 SERVINGS
PREP TIME: *20 minutes*
START TO FINISH: *1 hour 25 minutes*

3/4 cup all-purpose flour

1/2 cup granulated sugar

1 teaspoon baking powder

1 teaspoon ground cinnamon

1/4 teaspoon salt

1 1/2 cups coarsely chopped, peeled apples (1 1/2 medium)

1/2 cup slivered almonds

1/2 cup milk

3/4 cup packed brown sugar

1/4 cup butter or margarine

3/4 cup boiling water

Vanilla ice cream or whipped cream, if desired

1 Heat oven to 375°F. Grease 8-inch square (2-quart) glass baking dish or 1 1/2-quart casserole with shortening. In medium bowl, mix flour, granulated sugar, baking powder, cinnamon and salt. Add apples, almonds and milk; stir until well blended. Spread mixture in baking dish.

2 In small bowl, mix brown sugar, butter and boiling water until butter is melted. Pour over batter in baking dish.

3 Bake 45 to 50 minutes or until golden brown. Cool at least 15 minutes before serving. Serve with ice cream.

High Altitude (3500–6500 ft): No change.

1 Serving: Calories 390 (Calories from Fat 120); Total Fat 14g (Saturated Fat 6g; Trans Fat 0g); Cholesterol 20mg; Sodium 250mg; Total Carbohydrate 63g (Dietary Fiber 2g; Sugars 48g); Protein 5g **% Daily Value:** Vitamin A 6%; Vitamin C 0%; Calcium 15%; Iron 10% **Exchanges:** 1 1/2 Starch, 2 1/2 Other Carbohydrate, 2 1/2 Fat **Carbohydrate Choices:** 4

www.pillsbury.com

cobblers & crisps

incredible peach cobbler

BECKY BEUS
Kuna, ID
Bake-Off® Contest 39 • San Francisco, 2000

15 SERVINGS
PREP TIME: *15 minutes*
START TO FINISH: *1 hour 25 minutes*

½ cup butter or margarine

1 box (15.6 oz) cranberry quick bread
and muffin mix

2 tablespoons grated orange peel

2 cans (29 oz each) peach slices in
light syrup, drained, reserving
1 cup liquid

1 egg

⅓ cup sweetened dried cranberries

⅓ cup sugar

Vanilla ice cream, if desired

1 Heat oven to 375°F. Place butter in ungreased 13 × 9-inch pan. Place in oven until butter is melted; remove from oven.

2 Meanwhile, in large bowl, place quick bread mix, 1 tablespoon of the orange peel, 1 cup reserved peach liquid and the egg; stir 50 to 75 strokes with spoon until mix is moistened. Drop mixture by spoonfuls over butter in pan; spread slightly without stirring. Arrange peaches over mixture. Sprinkle with cranberries.

3 In small bowl, mix sugar and remaining tablespoon orange peel; sprinkle over fruit.

4 Bake 45 to 50 minutes or until edges are deep golden brown. Cool 20 minutes before serving. Serve warm with ice cream.

High Altitude (3500–6500 ft): Add 1 tablespoon all-purpose flour to dry quick bread mix.

1 Serving: Calories 260 (Calories from Fat 80); Total Fat 9g (Saturated Fat 4.5g; Trans Fat 1g); Cholesterol 30mg; Sodium 190mg; Total Carbohydrate 41g (Dietary Fiber 2g; Sugars 29g); Protein 3g **% Daily Value:** Vitamin A 15%; Vitamin C 4%; Calcium 0%; Iron 4% **Exchanges:** 1 Starch, 1 ½ Other Carbohydrate, 1 ½ Fat **Carbohydrate Choices:** 3

cherry-cinnamon cobbler

DORIS L. KELLER

Honolulu, HI

Bake-Off® Contest 12 • Washington, DC, 1960

6 SERVINGS

PREP TIME: *35 minutes*

START TO FINISH: *1 hour 5 minutes*

CINNAMON ROUNDS

1 ½ cups all-purpose flour

6 tablespoons packed brown sugar

1 ½ teaspoons baking powder

½ teaspoon salt

⅓ cup finely chopped pecans

⅓ cup shortening

1 egg

2 tablespoons milk

1 tablespoon butter or margarine, softened

¼ teaspoon ground cinnamon

FRUIT MIXTURE

½ cup granulated sugar

2 to 4 tablespoons red cinnamon candies

2 tablespoons cornstarch

½ cup water

1 can (14.5 oz) pitted tart cherries in water*

GLAZE

½ cup powdered sugar

1 tablespoon lemon juice

1 Heat oven to 400°F. In medium bowl, mix flour, 3 tablespoons of the brown sugar, the baking powder, salt and pecans. With pastry blender or fork, cut in shortening until mixture resembles coarse crumbs.

2 In small bowl, beat egg and milk with fork until blended. Add egg mixture to flour mixture; stir just until dry particles are moistened and dough forms (if necessary, add a few drops additional milk).

3 On floured surface, roll out dough into 14 × 12-inch rectangle. Brush with softened butter. In small bowl, mix remaining 3 tablespoons brown sugar and the cinnamon; sprinkle evenly over butter. Starting with one 12-inch side, roll up dough. Cut roll into 12 equal slices; set aside.

4 In 2-quart saucepan, mix granulated sugar, cinnamon candies and cornstarch. Stir in water. Drain cherries, reserving juice. Stir cherry juice into cornstarch mixture. Cook over medium heat 7 to 9 minutes, stirring occasionally, until thickened. Stir in cherries. Pour into ungreased 8-inch square (2-quart) glass baking dish. Arrange cinnamon rounds over fruit mixture.

5 Bake 25 to 30 minutes or until cinnamon rounds are no longer doughy. In small bowl, mix powdered sugar and lemon juice until smooth. Drizzle over warm cobbler. Cool at least 15 minutes before serving. Serve warm or cool.

High Altitude (3500–6500 ft): Bake 28 to 32 minutes.

See photo on page 89

One 14-ounce bag of frozen pitted cherries, thawed and reserving liquid, can be substituted for the canned cherries. Add enough water to the liquid to make ½ cup.

1 Serving: Calories 520 (Calories from Fat 170); Total Fat 19g (Saturated Fat 5g; Trans Fat 2g); Cholesterol 40mg; Sodium 350mg; Total Carbohydrate 80g (Dietary Fiber 3g; Sugars 51g); Protein 6g **% Daily Value:** Vitamin A 4%; Vitamin C 4%; Calcium 10%; Iron 15% **Exchanges:** 2 Starch, 3 Other Carbohydrate, 3 ½ Fat **Carbohydrate Choices:** 5

easy crescent-apple cobbler

6 SERVINGS

PREP TIME: *20 minutes*

START TO FINISH: *1 hour 15 minutes*

KEVIN BELLHORN

Richmond, MI

Bake-Off® Contest 24 • Hollywood, 1973

1 Heat oven to 375°F. In large bowl, mix apples, granulated sugar, flour and 1 teaspoon of the cinnamon.

2 Separate crescent dough into 4 rectangles. Press 2 rectangles in bottom of ungreased 8- or 9-inch square pan. Spread apple mixture over dough. Place remaining 2 rectangles over apples, gently stretching to cover.

3 In small bowl, mix brown sugar and remaining teaspoon cinnamon; sprinkle over dough. Drizzle with butter.

4 Bake 30 to 40 minutes or until deep golden brown and center is no longer doughy. Cool 15 minutes before serving. Serve with whipped cream.

High Altitude (3500–6500 ft): No change.

4 cups sliced peeled cooking apples (4 medium)

1/2 cup granulated sugar

3 tablespoons all-purpose flour

2 teaspoons ground cinnamon

1 can (8 oz) refrigerated crescent dinner rolls

1/2 cup packed brown sugar

2 tablespoons butter or margarine, melted

Whipped cream or vanilla ice cream, if desired

1 Serving: Calories 370 (Calories from Fat 110); Total Fat 12g (Saturated Fat 5g; Trans Fat 2g); Cholesterol 10mg; Sodium 330mg; Total Carbohydrate 62g (Dietary Fiber 2g; Sugars 44g); Protein 3g **% Daily Value:** Vitamin A 2%; Vitamin C 2%; Calcium 4%; Iron 8% **Exchanges:** 1 Starch, 3 Other Carbohydrate, 2 1/2 Fat **Carbohydrate Choices:** 4

cranberry-pear cobbler

MARSHA MICHAEL
Bloomington, MN
Bake-Off® Contest 38 • Orlando, 1998

10 SERVINGS
PREP TIME: *10 minutes*
START TO FINISH: *50 minutes*

FRUIT MIXTURE

2 cans (15 oz each) pear halves or
  slices, drained, liquid reserved
$^1/_2$ cup sweetened dried cranberries
$^1/_2$ cup applesauce
$^1/_4$ teaspoon ground cinnamon

TOPPING

$^1/_2$ cup sugar
$^1/_2$ teaspoon ground cinnamon
1 can (12 oz) refrigerated buttermilk
  biscuits
2 $^1/_2$ teaspoons butter or margarine

SERVE WITH, IF DESIRED

Vanilla ice cream or whipped cream

1 Heat oven to 450°F. Cut pears into 1-inch chunks. In ungreased 11 × 7-inch or 8-inch square (2-quart) glass baking dish, arrange pear chunks. Sprinkle with cranberries. In small bowl, mix applesauce and $^1/_4$ teaspoon cinnamon. Spoon over fruit.

2 Bake 8 to 10 minutes or until hot and bubbly. Remove from oven. Reduce oven temperature to 400°F.

3 In small bowl, mix sugar and $^1/_2$ teaspoon cinnamon. Separate dough into 10 biscuits. Dip each biscuit into reserved pear liquid; coat all sides with sugar-cinnamon mixture. Arrange biscuits over hot fruit in 2 rows of 5 biscuits each. Top each biscuit with about $^1/_4$ teaspoon butter.

4 Bake 15 to 20 minutes or until biscuits are golden brown. Cool 10 minutes before serving. Serve warm with ice cream.

High Altitude (3500–6500 ft): No change.

1 Serving: Calories 230 (Calories from Fat 45); Total Fat 5g (Saturated Fat 1.5g; Trans Fat 1.5g); Cholesterol 0mg; Sodium 370mg; Total Carbohydrate 43g (Dietary Fiber 2g; Sugars 27g); Protein 2g **% Daily Value:** Vitamin A 0%; Vitamin C 0%; Calcium 0%; Iron 6% **Exchanges:** 1 Starch, 1 Fruit, 1 Other Carbohydrate, $^1/_2$ Fat **Carbohydrate Choices:** 3

hidden glory cobbler

JAMES N. HOLEMAN

Sturgis, KY

Bake-Off® Contest 11 • Los Angeles, 1959

8 SERVINGS

PREP TIME: *35 minutes*

START TO FINISH: *1 hour 10 minutes*

1 Heat oven to 425°F. In large bowl, mix flour, 2 tablespoons sugar, the baking powder and salt. With pastry blender or fork, cut in shortening until particles are size of small peas. Sprinkle milk over flour mixture, tossing lightly with fork until dough is just moist enough to hold together. Reserve $1/3$ of dough for topping; shape remaining dough into ball.

2 On floured work surface, flatten ball to about $1/2$-inch thickness. Roll out dough into 10-inch square. Fit dough loosely into ungreased 8-inch square (2-quart) glass baking dish, pushing dough up sides of dish until even with top edges.

3 In 3-quart saucepan, mix 1 cup sugar, the tapioca, cornstarch, cherries with juice, frozen rhubarb and food color. Cook over medium-high heat, stirring occasionally, until mixture comes to a full boil. Pour into dough-lined baking dish. Dot with butter.

4 Shape remaining dough into ball. Roll out dough to about $1/4$-inch thickness. With 2 $1/2$-inch round cutter, cut dough into 8 rounds. Arrange dough rounds over fruit mixture. Sprinkle lightly with sugar.

5 Bake 15 to 20 minutes or until crust is golden brown. Cool at least 15 minutes before serving. Serve warm or cool with whipped cream.

High Altitude (3500–6500 ft): Decrease baking powder to 1 $1/2$ teaspoons; increase cornstarch to 2 tablespoons. In step 3, cook sugar mixture over medium-high heat until it comes to a full boil, then boil and stir 1 minute. Bake 20 to 25 minutes.

CRUST AND TOPPING

1 $1/2$ cups all-purpose flour

2 tablespoons sugar

2 teaspoons baking powder

$1/2$ teaspoon salt

$1/2$ cup shortening

6 to 7 tablespoons milk

Sugar

FRUIT MIXTURE

1 cup sugar

2 tablespoons quick-cooking tapioca

1 tablespoon cornstarch

1 can (14.5 oz) pitted tart cherries in water, undrained

1 bag (16 oz) frozen rhubarb

1 to 2 drops red food color

2 tablespoons butter or margarine

SERVE WITH, IF DESIRED

Whipped cream or ice cream

1 Serving: Calories 400 (Calories from Fat 150); Total Fat 16g (Saturated Fat 5g; Trans Fat 2.5g); Cholesterol 10mg; Sodium 300mg; Total Carbohydrate 58g (Dietary Fiber 2g; Sugars 35g); Protein 4g **% Daily Value:** Vitamin A 4%; Vitamin C 4%; Calcium 20%; Iron 8% **Exchanges:** 1 Starch, $1/2$ Fruit, 2 $1/2$ Other Carbohydrate, 3 Fat **Carbohydrate Choices:** 4

microwave honey-apple cobbler

JAMES SLOBODEN
Puyallup, WA
Bake-Off® Contest 32 • Orlando, 1986

8 SERVINGS
PREP TIME: *25 minutes*
START TO FINISH: *30 minutes*

FRUIT MIXTURE
4 cups thinly sliced, peeled cooking apples (4 medium)
$1/2$ cup packed brown sugar
1 teaspoon cornstarch
$1/2$ teaspoon ground cinnamon
2 tablespoons water
1 tablespoon lemon juice

CAKE
$1/2$ cup buttermilk*
$1/4$ cup honey
2 tablespoons vegetable oil
1 egg
1 cup all-purpose flour
$1/4$ cup packed brown sugar
$1/2$ teaspoon baking soda
$1/2$ teaspoon ground ginger
$1/4$ teaspoon baking powder
$1/4$ teaspoon salt
$1/4$ teaspoon ground nutmeg

GARNISH, IF DESIRED
Whipped cream

1 In 8-inch round (1 $1/2$-quart) microwavable dish or 2-quart round microwavable casserole, gently mix apples, $1/2$ cup brown sugar, the cornstarch, cinnamon, water and lemon juice. Cover with microwavable plastic wrap. Microwave on High 4 minutes, stirring once after 2 minutes, until apples are tender. Spread apples evenly in bottom of pan.

2 In small bowl, beat buttermilk, honey, oil and egg with electric mixer on medium speed until smooth. On low speed, beat in all remaining cake ingredients until well combined. Beat on medium speed 2 minutes. Pour batter over apples; tap pan on counter so batter settles evenly over apples.

3 Elevate dish on inverted microwavable dish or on shelf provided. Microwave on High 6 to 10 minutes, rotating dish $1/4$ turn every 2 minutes. Cake is done when toothpick inserted in center comes out clean and cake pulls away from sides of pan. Let stand on flat surface 5 minutes before serving. Serve warm or cool topped with whipped cream. Store cobbler in refrigerator.

High Altitude (3500–6500 ft): No change.

To substitute for buttermilk, use 1 $1/2$ teaspoons vinegar or lemon juice plus milk to make $1/2$ cup.

1 Serving: Calories 250 (Calories from Fat 40); Total Fat 4.5g (Saturated Fat 1g; Trans Fat 0g); Cholesterol 25mg; Sodium 200mg; Total Carbohydrate 49g (Dietary Fiber 1g; Sugars 35g); Protein 3g **% Daily Value:** Vitamin A 0%; Vitamin C 2%; Calcium 6%; Iron 8% **Exchanges:** 1 Starch, $1/2$ Fruit, 1 $1/2$ Other Carbohydrate, 1 Fat **Carbohydrate Choices:** 3

hot buttered rum and apple cobbler

MARGI MULKEY

Boise, ID

Bake-Off® Contest 30 • San Antonio, 1982

8 SERVINGS

PREP TIME: *20 minutes*

START TO FINISH: *1 hour 10 minutes*

COBBLER

1 cup all-purpose flour

$^3/_4$ cup sugar

2 teaspoons baking powder

$^1/_4$ teaspoon salt

$^1/_4$ cup butter or margarine, softened

$^1/_2$ cup milk

1 can (21 oz) apple pie filling

$^1/_3$ cup raisins

$^1/_2$ cup frozen (thawed) apple juice concentrate (from 12-oz can)

$^1/_2$ cup water

TOPPING

1 tablespoon sugar

1 teaspoon cornstarch

$^1/_4$ cup frozen (thawed) apple juice concentrate (from 12-oz can)

1 tablespoon butter or margarine

$^1/_2$ to 1 $^1/_2$ teaspoons rum extract

GARNISH, IF DESIRED

Whipped cream

1 Heat oven to 375°F. Grease 12 × 8-inch (2-quart) glass baking dish or 11 × 7-inch pan with shortening. In small bowl, mix flour, $^1/_2$ cup of the sugar, the baking powder, salt, $^1/_4$ cup butter and the milk with electric mixer on low speed until moistened, scraping bowl occasionally. Beat on high speed 1 minute. Spread in baking dish.

2 Spoon pie filling evenly over batter; sprinkle with raisins. Sprinkle with $^1/_4$ cup sugar; pour $^1/_2$ cup apple juice concentrate and the water over sugar.

3 Bake 40 to 50 minutes or until golden brown and toothpick inserted in cake portion comes out clean, covering with foil during last 10 minutes of baking if necessary to prevent excessive browning.

4 In 1-quart saucepan, blend 1 tablespoon sugar, the cornstarch, $^1/_4$ cup apple juice concentrate and 1 tablespoon butter over medium heat, stirring constantly, until thickened. Stir in rum extract. Pour and spread evenly over hot cobbler. Serve warm topped with whipped cream.

High Altitude (3500–6500 ft): No change.

1 Serving: Calories 480 (Calories from Fat 70); Total Fat 8g (Saturated Fat 5g; Trans Fat 0g); Cholesterol 20mg; Sodium 280mg; Total Carbohydrate 100g (Dietary Fiber 2g; Sugars 70g); Protein 3g **% Daily Value:** Vitamin A 6%; Vitamin C 6%; Calcium 10%; Iron 8% **Exchanges:** 1 Starch, 5 $^1/_2$ Other Carbohydrate, 1 $^1/_2$ Fat **Carbohydrate Choices:** 6 $^1/_2$

apple-cheddar-crescent cobbler

12 SERVINGS

PREP TIME: *35 minutes*

START TO FINISH: *1 hour*

FLAVIN GLOVER (MRS. GLENN)

Auburn, AL

Bake-Off® Contest 29 • Miami, 1980

1 Heat oven to 375°F. In 3-quart saucepan, mix sugar, cornstarch, cinnamon and salt. Stir in water. Add apples; cook over medium heat, stirring occasionally, until mixture boils. Reduce heat to low; simmer uncovered 2 minutes, stirring occasionally. Remove from heat. Stir in $1/2$ cup of the cheese. Pour apple mixture into ungreased 13 × 9-inch (3-quart) glass baking dish.

2 On work surface, unroll dough; separate into 2 long rectangles. Press dough into 13 × 9-inch rectangle; firmly press perforations to seal. Place dough rectangle over apple mixture; press to edges of baking dish.

3 In small bowl, mix remaining $1/2$ cup cheese, the nuts and butter; spoon evenly over dough.

4 Bake 18 to 22 minutes or until top is golden brown. Serve warm with ice cream.

High Altitude (3500–6500 ft): No change.

1 cup sugar

2 tablespoons cornstarch

1 teaspoon ground cinnamon

Dash salt

1 cup water

6 cups sliced peeled apples (6 medium)

1 cup shredded Cheddar cheese (4 oz)

1 can (8 oz) refrigerated crescent dinner rolls

$1/2$ cup chopped nuts

1 to 3 tablespoons butter or margarine, melted

Vanilla ice cream, if desired

1 Serving: Calories 250 (Calories from Fat 100); Total Fat 11g (Saturated Fat 4.5g; Trans Fat 1g); Cholesterol 10mg; Sodium 220mg; Total Carbohydrate 33g (Dietary Fiber 1g; Sugars 24g); Protein 5g **% Daily Value:** Vitamin A 2%; Vitamin C 0%; Calcium 6%; Iron 4% **Exchanges:** 1 $1/2$ Starch, $1/2$ Fruit, 2 Fat **Carbohydrate Choices:** 2

peach-berry cobbler

OLIVER C. DUFFINA
Washington, DC
Bake-Off® Contest 13 • Los Angeles, 1961

6 SERVINGS

PREP TIME: *20 minutes*
START TO FINISH: *1 hour 20 minutes*

FRUIT MIXTURE

$1/4$ cup granulated sugar

$1/4$ cup packed brown sugar

1 tablespoon cornstarch

$1/2$ cup water

1 tablespoon lemon juice

2 cups sliced peeled fresh peaches
   (3 medium) or frozen (thawed)
   unsweetened sliced peaches

1 cup fresh or frozen blueberries

TOPPING

1 cup all-purpose flour

$1/2$ cup granulated sugar

1 $1/2$ teaspoons baking powder

$1/2$ teaspoon salt

$1/2$ cup milk

$1/4$ cup butter or margarine, softened

2 tablespoons granulated sugar

$1/4$ teaspoon ground nutmeg

1 Heat oven to 375°F. In 3-quart saucepan, mix $1/4$ cup granulated sugar, the brown sugar and cornstarch. Stir in water. Cook over medium heat 7 to 9 minutes, stirring constantly, until thickened. Stir in lemon juice, peaches and blueberries. Pour into ungreased 8-inch square (2-quart) glass baking dish.

2 In medium bowl, mix flour, $1/2$ cup granulated sugar, the baking powder and salt. With electric mixer on medium speed, beat in milk and butter until smooth. Spoon over fruit mixture. Sprinkle with 2 tablespoons granulated sugar and the nutmeg.

3 Bake 40 to 45 minutes or until golden brown. Cool at least 15 minutes before serving. Serve warm or cool.

High Altitude (3500–6500 ft): No change.

1 Serving: Calories 350 (Calories from Fat 80); Total Fat 9g (Saturated Fat 5g; Trans Fat 0g); Cholesterol 20mg; Sodium 390mg; Total Carbohydrate 66g (Dietary Fiber 2g; Sugars 46g); Protein 4g **% Daily Value:** Vitamin A 10%; Vitamin C 6%; Calcium 10%; Iron 8% **Exchanges:** 1 Starch, $1/2$ Fruit, 3 Other Carbohydrate, 1 $1/2$ Fat **Carbohydrate Choices:** 4 $1/2$

caramel apple cobbler

MARGARET BLAKELY
New Philadelphia, OH
Bake-Off® Contest 27 • Boston, 1976

10 SERVINGS
PREP TIME: *25 minutes*
START TO FINISH: *50 minutes*

3 cups chunky applesauce
(from 48-oz jar)

1 jar (12 oz) caramel topping (1 cup)

³/₄ cup coconut

¹/₄ cup sugar

1 can (12 oz) refrigerated original
or buttermilk flaky biscuits

3 tablespoons butter or margarine,
melted

Vanilla ice cream or whipped cream,
if desired

1 Heat oven to 400°F. In ungreased 13 × 9-inch (3-quart) glass baking dish, mix applesauce and caramel topping.

2 Bake 10 to 15 minutes or until hot and bubbly around edges. Meanwhile, in small bowl, mix coconut and sugar.

3 Remove baking dish from oven. Separate dough into 10 biscuits. Cut each in half crosswise. Dip each biscuit half in melted butter; roll in coconut mixture to coat. Arrange biscuit halves, cut side down, over hot applesauce mixture. Sprinkle any remaining coconut mixture over biscuits.

4 Bake 20 to 25 minutes longer or until biscuits are golden brown. Serve warm with ice cream.

High Altitude (3500–6500 ft): In step 2, bake 15 to 20 minutes.

1 Serving: Calories 330 (Calories from Fat 90); Total Fat 10g (Saturated Fat 5g; Trans Fat 1.5g); Cholesterol 10mg; Sodium 520mg; Total Carbohydrate 59g (Dietary Fiber 1g; Sugars 39g); Protein 3g **% Daily Value:** Vitamin A 2%; Vitamin C 0%; Calcium 2%; Iron 6% **Exchanges:** 1 Starch, 3 Other Carbohydrate, 1 ¹/₂ Fat **Carbohydrate Choices:** 4

perky pear cobbler

MEREDITH S. PRESSEY
Marblehead, MA

Bake-Off® Contest 05 • New York City, 1953

8 SERVINGS

PREP TIME: *25 minutes*
START TO FINISH: *1 hour 10 minutes*

1 Heat oven to 400°F. To reserved pear syrup, add enough water to make 2 cups liquid. In ungreased 8-inch square or 9-inch round (2-quart) glass baking dish, arrange pear halves cut sides up; set aside.

2 In 2-quart saucepan, mix brown sugar, $1/4$ cup flour, $1/4$ teaspoon salt, the lemon peel and ginger. Gradually stir in pear liquid. Cook over medium-high heat 3 to 5 minutes, stirring constantly, until thickened. Stir in 1 tablespoon butter. Pour over pears.

3 In medium bowl, mix 1 cup flour, the baking powder and $1/2$ teaspoon salt. With pastry blender or fork, cut in 2 tablespoons butter until particles are size of small peas. In small bowl, beat egg and milk until blended. Add egg mixture all at once to flour mixture, stirring just until all dry particles are moistened.

4 On well-floured work surface, pat dough to $1/2$-inch thickness. With 2 $1/2$-inch round cutter, cut dough into rounds. Arrange dough rounds over fruit mixture; sprinkle nuts between rounds.

5 Bake 25 to 30 minutes or until biscuits are golden brown and bottoms are no longer doughy. Cool at least 15 minutes before serving. Serve warm garnished with additional lemon peel.

High Altitude (3500–6500 ft): No change.

FRUIT MIXTURE

6 pear halves (from 29-oz can), drained, reserving heavy syrup from can
Water
$1/4$ cup packed brown sugar
$1/4$ cup all-purpose flour
$1/4$ teaspoon salt
$1/2$ teaspoon grated lemon peel
Dash ground ginger
1 tablespoon butter or margarine

BISCUIT TOPPING

1 cup all-purpose flour
1 teaspoon baking powder
$1/2$ teaspoon salt
2 tablespoons butter or margarine
1 egg
$1/4$ cup milk
$1/4$ cup chopped nuts

GARNISH, IF DESIRED

Additional grated lemon peel

1 Serving: Calories 260 (Calories from Fat 70); Total Fat 8g (Saturated Fat 3.5g; Trans Fat 0g); Cholesterol 40mg; Sodium 330mg; Total Carbohydrate 42g (Dietary Fiber 3g; Sugars 23g); Protein 4g **% Daily Value:** Vitamin A 4%; Vitamin C 0%; Calcium 6%; Iron 8% **Exchanges:** 1 Starch, $1/2$ Fruit, 1 $1/2$ Other Carbohydrate, 1 $1/2$ Fat **Carbohydrate Choices:** 3

cherry-nut-crescent crisp

BETTY CHROMZACK

Northlake, IL

Bake-Off® Contest 23 • Houston, 1972

12 SERVINGS

PREP TIME: *15 minutes*

START TO FINISH: *55 minutes*

1 cup all-purpose flour

³/₄ cup chopped pecans

¹/₂ cup granulated sugar

¹/₂ cup packed brown sugar

1 teaspoon ground cinnamon

¹/₂ cup butter or margarine, softened

2 cans (8 oz each) refrigerated
crescent dinner rolls

1 can (21 oz) cherry pie filling

Powdered sugar, if desired

1 Heat oven to 375°F. In medium bowl, mix flour, pecans, granulated sugar, brown sugar, cinnamon and butter until crumbly. Sprinkle ¹/₃ of crumb mixture evenly in bottom of ungreased 13 × 9-inch pan.

2 Separate both cans of dough into 4 long rectangles. Place 3 rectangles over crumb mixture in pan; bring dough 1 inch up sides of pan to form crust. Sprinkle half of remaining crumb mixture over dough.

3 Spoon pie filling into crust. Sprinkle with remaining crumb mixture. Cut remaining dough rectangle into strips; place diagonally over pie filling to form a crisscross pattern.

4 Bake 30 to 40 minutes or until golden brown. Sprinkle with powdered sugar; serve warm.

High Altitude (3500–6500 ft): No change.

1 Serving: Calories 420 (Calories from Fat 190); Total Fat 21g (Saturated Fat 8g; Trans Fat 2.5g); Cholesterol 20mg; Sodium 350mg; Total Carbohydrate 53g (Dietary Fiber 2g; Sugars 31g); Protein 5g **% Daily Value:** Vitamin A 6%; Vitamin C 2%; Calcium 4%; Iron 10% **Exchanges:** 1 ¹/₂ Starch, 2 Other Carbohydrate, 4 Fat **Carbohydrate Choices:** 3 ¹/₂

chocolate-cherry crisp

AMY HEYD

Cincinnati, OH

Bake-Off® Contest 39 • San Francisco, 2000

10 SERVINGS

PREP TIME: *10 minutes*

START TO FINISH: *1 hour 35 minutes*

1 box (15.8 oz) double chocolate
   premium brownie mix with
   chocolate syrup
1 cup quick-cooking oats
$^1/_2$ cup chopped walnuts, if desired
$^1/_2$ cup butter or margarine, melted
2 cans (21 oz each) cherry pie filling
Vanilla ice cream
Fresh mint sprigs, if desired

1 Heat oven to 350°F. Reserve chocolate syrup packet from brownie mix for top-ping. In large bowl, mix brownie mix, oats and walnuts. Stir in butter until mix is moistened (mixture will be dry).

2 Spoon pie filling evenly into ungreased 8-inch square (2-quart) glass baking dish. Sprinkle brownie mixture over pie filling.

3 Bake 30 to 40 minutes or until edges are bubbly. Cool 45 minutes before serv-ing. Spoon crisp into dessert bowls. Top each serving with ice cream; drizzle with chocolate syrup from packet. Garnish with mint sprigs.

High Altitude (3500–6500 ft): No change.

1 Serving: Calories 500 (Calories from Fat 170); Total Fat 19g (Saturated Fat 10g; Trans Fat 1.5g); Cholesterol 40mg; Sodium 210mg; Total Carbohydrate 78g (Dietary Fiber 5g; Sugars 57g); Protein 5g **% Daily Value:** Vitamin A 10%; Vitamin C 6%; Calcium 6%; Iron 10% **Exchanges:** 1 $^1/_2$ Starch, 3 $^1/_2$ Other Carbohydrate, 3 $^1/_2$ Fat **Carbohydrate Choices:** 5

applescotch crisp

FRANK DONELSON
Bloomington, IL
Bake-Off® Contest 22 • Honolulu, 1971

8 SERVINGS

PREP TIME: *15 minutes*
START TO FINISH: *1 hour 5 minutes*

1 Heat oven to 350°F. In medium bowl, mix all topping ingredients until crumbly; set aside.

2 In large bowl, mix all fruit mixture ingredients. Pour into ungreased 9-inch square pan. Sprinkle topping over fruit mixture.

3 Bake 45 to 50 minutes or until apples are tender and topping is golden brown. Serve warm or cool.

High Altitude (3500–6500 ft): Heat oven to 375°F.

TOPPING

$^2/_3$ cup all-purpose flour

$^1/_2$ cup quick-cooking oats

$^1/_2$ cup chopped nuts

$^1/_4$ cup granulated sugar

$^1/_2$ teaspoon salt

1 teaspoon ground cinnamon

1 box (4-serving size) butterscotch or vanilla pudding and pie filling mix (not instant)

$^1/_2$ cup butter or margarine, melted

FRUIT MIXTURE

4 cups sliced peeled cooking apples (4 medium)

$^1/_2$ cup packed brown sugar

1 tablespoon all-purpose flour

$^1/_4$ cup milk

$^1/_2$ cup water

1 Serving: Calories 370 (Calories from Fat 150); Total Fat 17g (Saturated Fat 8g; Trans Fat 0.5g); Cholesterol 30mg; Sodium 310mg; Total Carbohydrate 51g (Dietary Fiber 2g; Sugars 34g); Protein 4g **% Daily Value:** Vitamin A 8%; Vitamin C 0%; Calcium 4%; Iron 8% **Exchanges:** 1 Starch, $^1/_2$ Fruit, 2 Other Carbohydrate, 3 Fat **Carbohydrate Choices:** 3 $^1/_2$

butter-peach crisp

JAMES F. WHITEMORE

Keene, NH

Bake-Off® Contest 12 • Washington, DC, 1960

8 SERVINGS

PREP TIME: *30 minutes*

START TO FINISH: *2 hours 5 minutes*

FRUIT MIXTURE

5 cups sliced peeled fresh peaches
(6 to 7 medium)

$1/4$ cup all-purpose flour

$1/3$ cup packed brown sugar

$1/2$ teaspoon ground cinnamon

$1/4$ teaspoon ground nutmeg

$1/2$ cup water

TOPPING

1 cup all-purpose flour

1 cup granulated sugar

1 teaspoon baking powder

$1/2$ teaspoon salt

$1/4$ teaspoon ground nutmeg

1 egg, slightly beaten

$1/2$ cup butter, melted

SAUCE

1 package (8 oz) cream cheese,
softened

2 tablespoons granulated sugar

2 tablespoons whipping cream

1 tablespoon grated orange peel
(1 medium)

2 tablespoons orange juice

1 Heat oven to 350°F. In ungreased 11 × 7-inch or 8-inch square (2-quart) glass baking dish, place peach slices. In small bowl, mix remaining fruit mixture ingredients until well blended. Stir into peaches.

2 In medium bowl, mix 1 cup flour, 1 cup granulated sugar, the baking powder, salt and $1/4$ teaspoon nutmeg. With fork, stir in egg until crumbly. Sprinkle over fruit mixture. Drizzle melted butter over top.

3 Bake 1 hour 10 minutes to 1 hour 20 minutes or until center is no longer doughy. Cool at least 15 minutes before serving.

4 Meanwhile, in small bowl, beat cream cheese with electric mixer on medium speed until fluffy. On low speed, beat in remaining sauce ingredients until smooth. Serve sauce with warm crisp.

High Altitude (3500–6500 ft): No change.

1 Serving: Calories 490 (Calories from Fat 210); Total Fat 24g (Saturated Fat 15g; Trans Fat 1g); Cholesterol 90mg; Sodium 390mg; Total Carbohydrate 64g (Dietary Fiber 2g; Sugars 47g); Protein 6g **% Daily Value:** Vitamin A 25%; Vitamin C 8%; Calcium 8%; Iron 10% **Exchanges:** 2 Starch, $1/2$ Fruit, 1 $1/2$ Other Carbohydrate, 4 $1/2$ Fat **Carbohydrate Choices:** 4

maple-applesauce cobbler cake

KIMBERLY A. CORDAS
Chesterland, OH
Bake-Off® Contest 37 • Dallas, 1996

8 SERVINGS
PREP TIME: *10 minutes*
START TO FINISH: *1 hour 5 minutes*

CAKE

1 tablespoon butter or margarine, softened

2 tablespoons packed brown sugar

1/4 teaspoon ground cinnamon

1/2 cup applesauce

2 tablespoons maple-flavored syrup

1 can (16.3 oz) large refrigerated buttermilk or original flaky biscuits

1/4 cup golden raisins

1/4 cup chopped pecans

TOPPING

1 1/2 cups applesauce

1/2 cup maple-flavored syrup

2 cups frozen (thawed) whipped topping

1 Heat oven to 350°F. Grease 9-inch round cake or square pan with 1 tablespoon butter. In small bowl, mix brown sugar, cinnamon, 1/2 cup applesauce and 2 tablespoons syrup until well blended.

2 Separate dough into 8 biscuits. Cut each biscuit into 8 pieces; place in pan. Sprinkle raisins and pecans over biscuit pieces. Spoon applesauce mixture over raisins and pecans.

3 Bake 35 to 45 minutes or until deep golden brown. Cool 10 minutes.

4 Meanwhile, in 2-quart saucepan, cook 1 1/2 cups applesauce and 1/2 cup syrup over low heat, stirring constantly, until thoroughly heated.

5 To serve, spoon warm cake into individual serving dishes. Spoon 1/4 cup applesauce mixture over each serving; top each with whipped topping. Store cake in refrigerator.

High Altitude (3500–6500 ft): No change.

1 Serving: Calories 430 (Calories from Fat 140); Total Fat 15g (Saturated Fat 7g; Trans Fat 3g); Cholesterol 0mg; Sodium 650mg; Total Carbohydrate 68g (Dietary Fiber 2g; Sugars 33g); Protein 5g **% Daily Value:** Vitamin A 0%; Vitamin C 0%; Calcium 4%; Iron 10% **Exchanges:** 1 1/2 Starch, 3 Other Carbohydrate, 3 Fat **Carbohydrate Choices:** 4 1/2

blueberry-butter-crumb dessert

PATRICIA A. MALOY
Concord, NH
Bake-Off® Contest 31 • San Diego, 1984

8 SERVINGS

PREP TIME: *35 minutes*
START TO FINISH: *1 hour 20 minutes*

1 In 9-inch microwavable pie plate or 10-inch microwavable quiche dish, microwave butter on High 30 to 60 seconds or until melted. Stir in 2 cups of the dry cake mix. Microwave on High 3 to 5 minutes, stirring every minute, until light brown. Cool 15 minutes.

2 Crumble cake mix mixture into fine crumbs. Reserve ¹/₂ cup crumbs for topping; press remaining crumbs in bottom of pie plate to form crust.

3 In medium bowl, beat egg whites with electric mixer on high speed until stiff. In small bowl, mix sour cream and lemon juice. Fold sour cream mixture into beaten egg whites. Fold in remaining dry cake mix. Gently stir in 1 cup blueberries. Spoon batter evenly over crust.

4 Microwave on High 2 minutes. Rotate pie plate ¹/₂ turn; microwave 3 to 6 minutes longer or until top is set. Sprinkle with reserved crumbs. Cool 1 hour.

5 In 4-cup microwavable bowl or measuring cup, mix sugar and water. Microwave on High 3 minutes. Stir in 1 cup blueberries; microwave on High 3 minutes longer or until Hot, stirring every minute. Cut cake into wedges; serve with sauce.

High Altitude (3500–6500 ft): No change.

DESSERT

¹/₂ cup butter or margarine

1 box (18.25 oz) white cake mix with pudding

2 egg whites

¹/₂ cup sour cream

1 teaspoon lemon juice

1 cup fresh or frozen blueberries, thawed, well drained

SAUCE

¹/₄ cup sugar

¹/₂ cup water

1 cup fresh or frozen blueberries, thawed, well drained

1 Serving: Calories 450 (Calories from Fat 180); Total Fat 20g (Saturated Fat 11g, Trans Fat 2.5g); Cholesterol 40mg; Sodium 540mg; Total Carbohydrate 62g (Dietary Fiber 0g, Sugars 37g); Protein 5g **% Daily Value:** Vitamin A 10%; Vitamin C 4%; Calcium 8%; Iron 6% **Exchanges:** 1 ¹/₂ Starch, 2 ¹/₂ Other Carbohydrate, 4 Fat **Carbohydrate Choices:** 4

peaches and crescent crisp dessert

LAURI WYMAN

Pembina, ND

Bake-Off® Contest 22 • Honolulu, 1971

10 SERVINGS

PREP TIME: *20 minutes*
START TO FINISH: *50 minutes*

SUGAR MIXTURE
- ³/₄ cup packed brown sugar
- ³/₄ cup all-purpose flour
- ¹/₄ cup butter or margarine, softened
- 1 package (3 oz) cream cheese, softened
- ¹/₂ teaspoon ground cinnamon
- ¹/₂ teaspoon ground ginger

CRUST
- 1 can (8 oz) refrigerated crescent dinner rolls

FRUIT
- 1 can (29 oz) sliced peaches, drained, reserving 1 cup syrup (2 ¹/₂ cups peach slices)

TOPPING
- 1 tablespoon butter or margarine
- 1 tablespoon cornstarch or all-purpose flour
- ¹/₄ cup packed brown sugar
- Reserved 1 cup peach syrup

SERVE WITH, IF DESIRED
- Whipped cream

1 Heat oven to 375°F. In small bowl, mix all sugar mixture ingredients with fork until crumbly; set aside.

2 Separate dough into 4 rectangles; place in ungreased 12-inch pizza pan, 15 × 10 × 1-inch pan or on large cookie sheet. Press to form crust. Arrange peaches over crust; sprinkle with sugar mixture.

3 Bake 25 to 30 minutes or until crust is golden brown.

4 In 1-quart saucepan, melt 1 tablespoon butter. Stir in cornstarch until well blended. Stir in remaining topping ingredients. Cook about 5 minutes, stirring occasionally, until bubbly and thickened. Spoon topping over warm dessert. Serve warm or cool with whipped cream.

High Altitude (3500–6500 ft): In step 2, before topping crust with peaches and sugar mixture, prebake crust 5 minutes.

1 Serving: Calories 360 (Calories from Fat 120); Total Fat 14g (Saturated Fat 7g; Trans Fat 1.5g); Cholesterol 25mg; Sodium 260mg; Total Carbohydrate 55g (Dietary Fiber 2g; Sugars 37g); Protein 4g **% Daily Value:** Vitamin A 10%; Vitamin C 0%; Calcium 4%; Iron 10% **Exchanges:** 1 ¹/₂ Starch, 2 Other Carbohydrate, 2 ¹/₂ Fat **Carbohydrate Choices:** 3 ¹/₂

pastries

raspberry-crescent twists

MARY ANN MARIOTTI
Plainfield, IL
Bake-Off® Contest 41 • Hollywood, 2004

8 TWISTS
PREP TIME: *15 minutes*
START TO FINISH: *35 minutes*

TWISTS

1 can (8 oz) refrigerated regular or
reduced-fat crescent dinner rolls

$^1/_4$ cup red raspberry filling
(from 12-oz can)

$^1/_4$ cup sliced almonds, finely chopped

GLAZE

$^1/_2$ cup powdered sugar

$^1/_2$ teaspoon almond extract

1 to 2 teaspoons water

GARNISH, IF DESIRED

Additional sliced almonds

1 Heat oven to 375°F. Line 15 × 10 × 1-inch pan or large cookie sheet with parchment paper. Unroll dough on cutting board into 2 long rectangles; press each into 12 × 3 $^1/_2$-inch rectangle, firmly pressing perforations to seal.

2 Spread raspberry filling on 1 dough rectangle to within $^1/_2$ inch of all edges. Sprinkle evenly with chopped almonds. Place second dough rectangle over almonds; gently press top and long edges to seal. Cut crosswise into 8 strips. Twist each strip twice; place 2 inches apart in pan.

3 Bake 11 to 13 minutes or until deep golden brown. Remove twists from pan; place on wire rack. Cool 10 minutes. Meanwhile, in small bowl, blend powdered sugar, almond extract and enough water for desired spreading consistency until smooth.

4 Spread glaze over cooled twists; sprinkle with additional sliced almonds.

High Altitude (3500–6500 ft): Bake 13 to 15 minutes.

See photo on page 113

1 Twist: Calories 190 (Calories from Fat 70); Total Fat 8g (Saturated Fat 2g; Trans Fat 1.5g); Cholesterol 0mg; Sodium 220mg; Total Carbohydrate 26g (Dietary Fiber 0g; Sugars 14g); Protein 3g **% Daily Value:** Vitamin A 0%; Vitamin C 0%; Calcium 0%; Iron 4% **Exchanges:** 1 Starch, $^1/_2$ Other Carbohydrate, 1 $^1/_2$ Fat **Carbohydrate Choices:** 2

rich crescent-nut delights

12 SERVINGS

PREP TIME: *20 minutes*
START TO FINISH: *1 hour 20 minutes*

JOHN L. BUTLER
Milford, PA
Bake-Off® Contest 40 • Orlando, 2002

1 Heat oven to 375°F. In 2-quart saucepan, melt $^1/_4$ cup butter over medium heat. Add brown sugar; cook 3 minutes, stirring constantly. Reduce heat to low. Stir in pecans, walnuts, cinnamon, salt, honey and syrup. Cook 3 minutes, stirring occasionally. Remove from heat; stir in maple flavor. Cool 15 minutes.

2 Sprinkle 3 teaspoons of the flour over work surface. Unroll dough on floured surface; press perforations to seal. Sprinkle with remaining 2 teaspoons flour. With rolling pin, roll dough into 18 × 12-inch rectangle.

3 Carefully spoon and spread pecan mixture evenly over 1 long side of dough in 4-inch-wide strip, spreading to within $^1/_2$ inch of edges. Starting with topped side, carefully roll up dough (there may be small breaks in dough).

4 Spoon 1 tablespoon of the melted butter diagonally on ungreased large cookie sheet. Place filled roll, seam side down, over butter. Pinch ends to seal. Gently flatten dough until 3 inches wide. Brush top and sides with remaining tablespoon melted butter. Sprinkle with cinnamon-sugar.

5 Bake 16 to 18 minutes or until golden brown. Cool 25 minutes. Cut roll lengthwise into 2 long pieces; cut each half into 1-inch slices. Serve warm or cool.

High Altitude (3500–6500 ft): No change.

$^1/_4$ cup regular or unsalted butter

$^1/_3$ cup packed brown sugar

$^1/_2$ cup chopped pecans

$^1/_2$ cup chopped walnuts

$^1/_2$ teaspoon ground cinnamon

Dash salt

1 tablespoon honey

1 tablespoon real maple syrup or maple-flavored syrup

1 $^1/_2$ teaspoons imitation maple flavor

5 teaspoons all-purpose flour

1 can (8 oz) refrigerated crescent dinner rolls

2 tablespoons butter, melted

2 teaspoons cinnamon-sugar

1 Serving: Calories 230 (Calories from Fat 150); Total Fat 16g (Saturated Fat 6g; Trans Fat 1.5g); Cholesterol 15mg; Sodium 200mg; Total Carbohydrate 19g (Dietary Fiber 1g; Sugars 11g); Protein 3g **% Daily Value:** Vitamin A 4%; Vitamin C 0%; Calcium 2%; Iron 4% **Exchanges:** 1 Starch, $^1/_2$ Other Carbohydrate, 3 Fat **Carbohydrate Choices:** 1

cherry-almond swirls

JENNY RIEGSECKER

Delta, OH

Bake-Off® Contest 41 • Hollywood, 2004

12 ROLLS

PREP TIME: *20 minutes*

START TO FINISH: *40 minutes*

$1/4$ cup granulated sugar

$1/2$ cup slivered almonds

1 package (3 oz) cream cheese, softened, cut into pieces

$1/4$ teaspoon vanilla

$1/8$ teaspoon almond extract

1 egg yolk

1 can (8 oz) refrigerated crescent dinner rolls

$1/4$ cup cherry preserves

$1/2$ cup powdered sugar

2 teaspoons water

1 Heat oven to 375°F. Spray 12 regular-size muffin cups with cooking spray. In food processor, process granulated sugar and almonds about 30 seconds or until almonds are finely ground. Add cream cheese, vanilla, almond extract and egg yolk; process about 10 seconds or until well blended.

2 On lightly floured surface, unroll dough into 1 large rectangle. With floured rolling pin or fingers, roll or press dough into 12 × 9-inch rectangle, firmly pressing perforations to seal.

3 Spread cream cheese mixture evenly over dough rectangle. Starting with one long side, roll up dough into log (filling will be soft). With serrated knife, cut log into 12 slices; place cut side up in muffin cups.

4 Bake 11 to 15 minutes or until light golden brown. Remove rolls from oven. With handle of wooden spoon, make indentation in center of each roll; spoon 1 teaspoon preserves into each.

5 Bake 2 to 4 minutes longer or until golden brown. Run knife around edge of each muffin cup to loosen. Remove rolls from cups; place on wire racks.

6 In small bowl, blend powdered sugar and water until smooth; drizzle over warm rolls. Serve warm or cool. Store rolls in refrigerator.

High Altitude (3500–6500 ft): In step 4, bake 13 to 17 minutes.

1 Roll: Calories 180 (Calories from Fat 80); Total Fat 9g (Saturated Fat 3g; Trans Fat 1g); Cholesterol 25mg; Sodium 170mg; Total Carbohydrate 22g (Dietary Fiber 0g; Sugars 14g); Protein 3g **% Daily Value:** Vitamin A 2%; Vitamin C 0%; Calcium 2%; Iron 4% **Exchanges:** 1 Starch, $1/2$ Other Carbohydrate, 1 $1/2$ Fat **Carbohydrate Choices:** 1 $1/2$

tropic treasure chest pastry

12 SERVINGS

PREP TIME: *20 minutes*

START TO FINISH: *1 hour 5 minutes*

PATRICIA SCHROEDL

Jefferson, WI

Bake-Off® Contest 40 • Orlando, 2002

1 Heat oven to 375°F. In medium bowl, beat granulated sugar, butter and 1 teaspoon almond extract with electric mixer on medium speed until light and fluffy. Beat in flour until well blended. Stir in coconut, macadamia nuts, vanilla baking chips and cherries.

2 Remove 1 pie crust from pouch; unroll on ungreased cookie sheet. Spread coconut mixture to within 1 inch of edge of crust. Brush edge with beaten egg. Remove remaining pie crust from pouch; unroll crust and place over filling. Press and crimp edges to seal. Brush top with beaten egg.

3 Bake 18 to 26 minutes or until golden brown. Cool 15 minutes. Meanwhile, in small bowl, blend powdered sugar, $^1/_4$ teaspoon almond extract and enough milk for desired drizzling consistency until smooth.

4 Drizzle glaze over pastry. Cut into wedges; serve warm or cool.

High Altitude (3500–6500 ft): Bake 20 to 24 minutes.

FILLING AND CRUST

$^1/_2$ cup granulated sugar

$^1/_4$ cup butter or margarine, softened

1 teaspoon almond extract

$^1/_4$ cup all-purpose flour

$^1/_2$ cup coconut

$^1/_2$ cup chopped macadamia nuts

$^1/_2$ cup white vanilla baking chips

$^1/_2$ cup dried cherries

1 box (15 oz) refrigerated pie crusts, softened as directed on box

1 egg, beaten

GLAZE

$^1/_2$ cup powdered sugar

$^1/_4$ teaspoon almond extract

2 to 3 teaspoons milk

1 Serving: Calories 380 (Calories from Fat 190); Total Fat 21g (Saturated Fat 10g; Trans Fat 0g); Cholesterol 35mg; Sodium 220mg; Total Carbohydrate 45g (Dietary Fiber 0g; Sugars 24g); Protein 2g **% Daily Value:** Vitamin A 6%; Vitamin C 0%; Calcium 2%; Iron 2% **Exchanges:** 1 Starch, 2 Other Carbohydrate, 4 Fat **Carbohydrate Choices:** 3

strawberry–cream cheese pastries

BECKY KOYLE

Boise, ID

Bake-Off® Contest 41 • Hollywood, 2004

8 PASTRIES

PREP TIME: *20 minutes*

START TO FINISH: *50 minutes*

1 package (8 oz) cream cheese, softened

$^1/_2$ cup sugar

1 tablespoon whipping cream

$^1/_2$ teaspoon ground cinnamon

$^1/_2$ teaspoon grated lemon peel

1 teaspoon lemon juice

8 strawberry chewy fruit snack rolls (from 5-oz box)

2 cans (8 oz) refrigerated crescent dinner rolls

1 tablespoon milk

2 tablespoons sugar

1 Heat oven to 375°F. In medium bowl, beat cream cheese and $^1/_2$ cup sugar with electric mixer on medium speed until creamy. Beat in cream, cinnamon, lemon peel and lemon juice.

2 Remove fruit snack rolls from wrappers; fold each in half lengthwise.

3 Unroll both cans of dough; separate into 8 rectangles and firmly press perforations to seal. Place 1 folded fruit roll lengthwise down center of each dough rectangle.

4 Spoon 2 rounded tablespoons cream cheese mixture onto $^1/_2$ of each fruit snack roll; spread slightly. Fold dough rectangle in half crosswise. Place on ungreased cookie sheet; press edges with fork to seal. Brush tops with milk; sprinkle with 2 tablespoons sugar. With sharp knife, cut 3 diagonal slits in top of each square.

5 Bake 13 to 18 minutes or until deep golden brown. Cool on cookie sheet 10 minutes. Remove from cookie sheet; serve warm.

High Altitude (3500–6500 ft): Bake 15 to 18 minutes.

1 Pastry: Calories 430 (Calories from Fat 210); Total Fat 23g (Saturated Fat 11g; Trans Fat 3.5g); Cholesterol 35mg; Sodium 580mg; Total Carbohydrate 50g (Dietary Fiber 0g; Sugars 28g); Protein 6g **% Daily Value:** Vitamin A 8%; Vitamin C 15%; Calcium 4%; Iron 8% **Exchanges:** 1 $^1/_2$ Starch, 2 Other Carbohydrate, 4 $^1/_2$ Fat **Carbohydrate Choices:** 3

crescent-coconut-almond twist

JOAN PISERCHIO

Colonia, NJ

Bake-Off® Contest 40 • Orlando, 2002

8 SERVINGS

PREP TIME: *15 minutes*

START TO FINISH: *50 minutes*

TWIST

$^3/_4$ cup sliced almonds, toasted*

2 tablespoons packed brown sugar

1 tablespoon butter, softened

$^3/_4$ cup coconut

1 tablespoon all-purpose flour

1 teaspoon almond extract

1 egg, separated

1 can (8 oz) refrigerated crescent dinner rolls

2 teaspoons water

GLAZE

$^1/_3$ cup plus 1 tablespoon powdered sugar

2 teaspoons milk

$^1/_2$ teaspoon almond extract

1 Heat oven to 350°F. Grease cookie sheet with shortening. Reserve 1 tablespoon almonds for garnish. Place remaining almonds in food-storage plastic bag; crush with rolling pin.

2 In medium bowl, mix brown sugar and butter. Stir in crushed almonds, coconut, flour, 1 teaspoon almond extract and the egg white.

3 Unroll dough into 2 long rectangles; firmly press perforations to seal. Press each into 12 × 4-inch rectangle. Spread half of almond mixture in 2-inch-wide strip lengthwise down center of each rectangle to within $^1/_4$ inch of each end. Fold sides over filling; pinch edges to seal.

4 With rolls side by side and starting at one end, carefully overlap rolls 2 times to form 1 twist; press ends to seal. Place twist on cookie sheet. In small bowl, beat egg yolk and water with fork; brush over twist.

5 Bake 19 to 25 minutes or until golden brown. Cool 10 minutes. Remove from cookie sheet; place on wire rack.

6 In small bowl, blend all glaze ingredients until smooth; drizzle over twist. Garnish with reserved almonds. Cut into diagonal slices; serve warm or cool.

High Altitude (3500–6500 ft): No change.

To toast almonds, bake uncovered in ungreased shallow pan in 350°F oven about 10 minutes, stirring occasionally, until golden brown.

1 Serving: Calories 280 (Calories from Fat 150); Total Fat 16g (Saturated Fat 6g; Trans Fat 1.5g); Cholesterol 30mg; Sodium 260mg; Total Carbohydrate 27g (Dietary Fiber 2g; Sugars 15g); Protein 5g **% Daily Value:** Vitamin A 0%; Vitamin C 0%; Calcium 4%; Iron 8% **Exchanges:** 1 $^1/_2$ Starch, $^1/_2$ Other Carbohydrate, 3 Fat **Carbohydrate Choices:** 2

poppin' fresh® citrus-glazed crullers

12 ROLLS

PREP TIME: *15 minutes*
START TO FINISH: *40 minutes*

ERIKA COUCH
Ballston Spa, NY

Bake-Off® Contest 39 • San Francisco, 2000

1 Heat oven to 375°F. Line cookie sheet with parchment paper or spray with cooking spray. In shallow dish, place melted butter; in another shallow dish, place granulated sugar.

2 Unroll dough; separate into 12 breadsticks. Dip both sides of each breadstick in butter; coat with sugar. Twist each breadstick; place on cookie sheet, pressing ends down firmly.

3 Bake 13 to 17 minutes or until golden brown. Meanwhile, in small bowl, blend all glaze ingredients until smooth.

4 Remove rolls from oven. Immediately drizzle glaze over rolls. Remove from cookie sheet; cool 5 minutes before serving.

High Altitude (3500–6500 ft): No change.

ROLLS

$1/4$ cup butter or margarine, melted

$1/2$ cup granulated sugar

1 can (11 oz) refrigerated original breadsticks

GLAZE

2/3 cup powdered sugar

$1/4$ teaspoon grated orange peel

$1/4$ teaspoon grated lemon peel

1 tablespoon orange juice

1 teaspoon lemon juice

1 Roll: Calories 160 (Calories from Fat 45); Total Fat 5g (Saturated Fat 2.5g; Trans Fat 0g); Cholesterol 10mg; Sodium 210mg; Total Carbohydrate 28g (Dietary Fiber 0g; Sugars 16g); Protein 2g **% Daily Value:** Vitamin A 2%; Vitamin C 0%; Calcium 0%; Iron 4% **Exchanges:** 1 Starch, $1/2$ Other Carbohydrate, 1 Fat **Carbohydrate Choices:** 2

viennese chocolate dream pastries

FLORENCE NEAVOLL

Salem, OR

Bake-Off® Contest 37 • Dallas, 1996

16 SERVINGS

PREP TIME: *35 minutes*

START TO FINISH: *2 hours 50 minutes*

CRUST

1 box (15 oz) refrigerated pie crusts, softened as directed on box

1 tablespoon butter, softened

1 tablespoon granulated sugar

$1/4$ teaspoon ground cinnamon

FILLING

4 oz cream cheese, softened

$1/4$ cup apricot preserves

$1/4$ teaspoon ground cinnamon

$1/8$ teaspoon salt

1 cup white vanilla baking chips

TOPPING

1 egg, beaten

1 teaspoon granulated sugar

CHOCOLATE GLAZE

3 oz semisweet baking chocolate, chopped

3 tablespoons water

1 tablespoon butter

1 cup powdered sugar

$1/2$ teaspoon vanilla

WHITE CHOCOLATE GLAZE

$1/4$ cup white vanilla baking chips

1 teaspoon shortening or vegetable oil

1. Heat oven to 425°F. Remove 1 pie crust from pouch; unroll on ungreased cookie sheet or 12-inch pizza pan. Spread 1 tablespoon butter over crust to within 1 inch of edge. In small bowl, mix 1 tablespoon granulated sugar and $1/4$ teaspoon cinnamon; sprinkle evenly over butter.

2. In small bowl, beat cream cheese until smooth. Beat in all remaining filling ingredients. Spoon and spread over sugar mixture on crust. Brush edge of crust lightly with water.

3. Unroll second pie crust; place over filling. Press edges together to seal; flute. Cut several slits in top crust for steam to escape. Brush with beaten egg; sprinkle with 1 teaspoon granulated sugar.

4. Bake 18 to 22 minutes or until crust is golden brown. Cool completely, about 1 hour 30 minutes.

5. Carefully remove pastry from cookie sheet; place on serving plate. In 1-quart saucepan, heat chocolate, water and 1 tablespoon butter over low heat, stirring occasionally, until chocolate is melted and mixture is smooth. With wire whisk, beat in powdered sugar and vanilla until smooth. Spread over top of crust. Refrigerate 10 minutes.

6. In another 1-quart saucepan, heat $1/4$ cup vanilla baking chips and shortening over low heat, stirring occasionally, until melted and smooth. Drizzle over chocolate glaze. Cut into wedges. Store in refrigerator.

High Altitude (3500–6500 ft): In step 1, prebake bottom pie crust about 8 minutes. Do not spread 1 tablespoon butter over crust; sprinkle crust with sugar/cinnamon mixture and continue as directed. In step 4, bake 23 to 27 minutes, covering crust edge with foil during last 10 minutes of baking to prevent overbrowning.

1 Serving: Calories 330 (Calories from Fat 160); Total Fat 18g (Saturated Fat 10g; Trans Fat 0g); Cholesterol 30mg; Sodium 200mg; Total Carbohydrate 40g (Dietary Fiber 0g; Sugars 25g); Protein 2g **% Daily Value:** Vitamin A 4%; Vitamin C 0%; Calcium 4%; Iron 0% **Exchanges:** $1/2$ Starch, 2 Other Carbohydrate, 3 $1/2$ Fat **Carbohydrate Choices:** 2 $1/2$

easy danish kringle

DEAN PHILIPP
New York, NY
Bake-Off® Contest 38 • Orlando, 1998

8 SERVINGS
PREP TIME: *15 minutes*
START TO FINISH: *1 hour 15 minutes*

1 refrigerated pie crust (from 15-oz box), softened as directed on box

$2/3$ cup chopped pecans

$1/3$ cup packed brown sugar

3 tablespoons butter or margarine, softened

$1/2$ cup powdered sugar

$1/4$ teaspoon vanilla

2 to 3 teaspoons milk

3 tablespoons chopped pecans, if desired

1 Heat oven to 375°F. Remove pie crust from pouch; unroll on large ungreased cookie sheet.

2 In medium bowl, mix $2/3$ cup pecans, the brown sugar and butter. Sprinkle over half of pie crust to within $3/4$ inch of edge. Brush edge with water; fold crust over pecan mixture. Move to center of cookie sheet. Press edges with fork to seal; prick top with fork.

3 Bake 17 to 22 minutes or until golden brown. Cool 5 minutes.

4 In small bowl, blend powdered sugar, vanilla and enough milk for desired drizzling consistency until smooth. Drizzle over kringle; sprinkle with 3 tablespoons pecans. Cool 30 minutes before serving.

High Altitude (3500–6500 ft): No change.

1 Serving: Calories 290 (Calories from Fat 160); Total Fat 18g (Saturated Fat 6g; Trans Fat 0g); Cholesterol 15mg; Sodium 140mg; Total Carbohydrate 31g (Dietary Fiber 0g; Sugars 16g); Protein 0g **% Daily Value:** Vitamin A 2%; Vitamin C 0%; Calcium 0%; Iron 2% **Exchanges:** 2 Other Carbohydrate, 3 $1/2$ Fat **Carbohydrate Choices:** 2

easy crescent danish rolls

8 ROLLS

PREP TIME: *20 minutes*

START TO FINISH: *45 minutes*

BARBARA S. GIBSON

Ft. Wayne, IN

Bake-Off® Contest 26 • San Francisco, 1975

1 Heat oven to 350°F. In small bowl, beat cream cheese, granulated sugar and lemon juice with spoon until smooth. Separate dough into 8 rectangles; firmly press perforations to seal. Spread each rectangle with about 2 tablespoons cream cheese mixture.

2 Starting with one long side, roll up each rectangle; firmly press edges and ends to seal. Gently stretch each roll until about 10 inches long. Coil each roll into a spiral with seam on the inside, tucking end under. Make deep indentation in center of each roll; fill with $^1/_2$ teaspoon preserves. Place on ungreased large cookie sheet.

3 Bake 20 to 25 minutes or until deep golden brown.

4 In small bowl, blend all glaze ingredients until smooth, adding enough milk for desired drizzling consistency; drizzle over warm rolls. Serve warm. Store rolls in refrigerator.

High Altitude (3500–6500 ft): No change.

ROLLS

1 package (8 oz) cream cheese, softened

$^1/_2$ cup granulated sugar

1 tablespoon lemon juice

2 cans (8 oz each) refrigerated crescent dinner rolls

4 teaspoons preserves or jam (any flavor)

GLAZE

$^1/_2$ cup powdered sugar

1 teaspoon vanilla

2 to 3 teaspoons milk

1 Roll: Calories 400 (Calories from Fat 200); Total Fat 22g (Saturated Fat 10g; Trans Fat 4g); Cholesterol 30mg; Sodium 530mg; Total Carbohydrate 45g (Dietary Fiber 0g; Sugars 26g); Protein 6g **% Daily Value:** Vitamin A 8%; Vitamin C 0%; Calcium 4%; Iron 8% **Exchanges:** 2 Starch, 1 Other Carbohydrate, 4 Fat **Carbohydrate Choices:** 3

giant cinnamon-cheese danish

BETTY NICOSON

Terre Haute, IN

Bake-Off® Contest 41 • Hollywood, 2004

6 SERVINGS

PREP TIME: *15 minutes*

START TO FINISH: *55 minutes*

1 can (17.5 oz) large refrigerated
   cinnamon rolls with icing

1 package (8 oz) cream cheese,
   softened

¹/₂ cup sugar

2 teaspoons sour cream

1 teaspoon lemon juice

1 teaspoon vanilla

1 Heat oven to 350°F. Lightly grease 9-inch glass pie plate with shortening or cooking spray. Separate dough into 5 rolls; set icing aside. Unroll 1 roll into long strip of dough; reroll loosely and place in center of pie plate.

2 Unroll second roll; loosely wrap around first roll, cinnamon side in, replacing any cinnamon that falls off. Repeat with remaining rolls, coiling dough in pie plate into spiral shape.

3 In small bowl, beat all remaining ingredients with electric mixer on medium speed until smooth. Spoon cream cheese mixture into decorating bag with tip or gallon-size resealable food-storage plastic bag with ¹/₂-inch hole cut in bottom corner. With tip or corner of bag about halfway down into rolls, pipe mixture between strips of dough, starting at center and working to edge of pie plate, using all of mixture.

4 Bake 25 to 35 minutes or until center is thoroughly baked and edges are deep golden brown. Cool 5 minutes. Meanwhile, remove cover from icing; microwave on Medium (50%) 10 to 15 seconds or until drizzling consistency.

5 Drizzle icing over warm coffee cake. Cut into wedges; serve warm.

High Altitude (3500–6500 ft): No change.

1 Serving: Calories 480 (Calories from Fat 200); Total Fat 23g (Saturated Fat 11g; Trans Fat 3g); Cholesterol 45mg; Sodium 670mg; Total Carbohydrate 61g (Dietary Fiber 0g; Sugars 37g); Protein 7g **% Daily Value:** Vitamin A 10%; Vitamin C 0%; Calcium 4%; Iron 10% **Exchanges:** 2 Starch, 2 Other Carbohydrate, 4 ¹/₂ Fat **Carbohydrate Choices:** 4

magic marshmallow crescent puffs

EDNA M. WALKER

Eden Prairie, MN

Bake-Off® Contest 20 • Atlanta, 1969

16 ROLLS

PREP TIME: *20 minutes*

START TO FINISH: *35 minutes*

ROLLS

1/4 cup granulated sugar

2 tablespoons all-purpose flour

1 teaspoon ground cinnamon

2 cans (8 oz) refrigerated crescent dinner rolls

16 large marshmallows

1/4 cup butter or margarine, melted

GLAZE

1/2 cup powdered sugar

1/2 teaspoon vanilla

2 to 3 teaspoons milk

1 Heat oven to 375°F. Spray 16 regular-size muffin cups with cooking spray. In small bowl, mix granulated sugar, flour and cinnamon.

2 Separate dough into 16 triangles. For each roll, dip 1 marshmallow in melted butter; roll in sugar mixture. Place marshmallow on shortest side of triangle. Roll up, starting at shortest side and rolling to opposite point. Completely cover marshmallow with dough; firmly pinch edges to seal. Dip 1 end in remaining butter; place butter side down in muffin cup.

3 Bake 12 to 15 minutes or until golden brown (place sheet of foil or cookie sheet on oven rack below muffin cups to guard against spills). Cool rolls in pan 1 minute. Remove from muffin cups; place on wire racks set over sheet of waxed paper.

4 In small bowl, blend all glaze ingredients until smooth, adding enough milk for desired drizzling consistency; drizzle over warm rolls. Serve warm.

High Altitude (3500–6500 ft): No change.

1 Roll: Calories 190 (Calories from Fat 80); Total Fat 9g (Saturated Fat 4g; Trans Fat 1.5g); Cholesterol 10mg; Sodium 250mg; Total Carbohydrate 25g (Dietary Fiber 0g; Sugars 13g); Protein 2g **% Daily Value:** Vitamin A 0%; Vitamin C 0%; Calcium 0%; Iron 4% **Exchanges:** 1/2 Starch, 1 Other Carbohydrate, 2 Fat **Carbohydrate Choices:** 1 1/2

ruby razz crunch

C. W. MYERS

Fort Collins, CO

Bake-Off® Contest 08 • New York City, 1956

9 SERVINGS

PREP TIME: *25 minutes*

START TO FINISH: *1 hour 30 minutes*

FILLING

1 package (10 oz) frozen raspberries with syrup, thawed, drained, reserving liquid

1 bag (16 oz) frozen rhubarb, thawed, drained, reserving liquid

$1/2$ cup granulated sugar

3 tablespoons cornstarch

GARNISH

$1/2$ cup whipping cream, whipped

2 tablespoons granulated sugar

1 to 3 drops red food color, if desired

CRUST AND TOPPING

1 $1/4$ cups all-purpose flour

1 cup packed brown sugar

1 cup quick-cooking oats

1 teaspoon ground cinnamon

$1/2$ cup butter or margarine, melted

1 Heat oven to 325°F. Reserve 2 tablespoons raspberries for topping. In measuring cup, mix reserved raspberry and rhubarb liquids; if necessary, add water to make 1 cup.

2 In 2-quart saucepan, mix $1/2$ cup granulated sugar and the cornstarch; stir in reserved liquids. Cook over medium heat, stirring constantly, until thickened. Remove from heat. Stir in remaining raspberries and rhubarb; set aside.

3 Line cookie sheet with waxed paper. In small bowl, gently mix whipped cream, 2 tablespoons granulated sugar, reserved raspberries and food color. Drop in 9 mounds onto lined cookie sheet; freeze until firm.

4 In large bowl, mix flour, brown sugar, oats and cinnamon. Stir in butter until crumbly. Press $2/3$ of crumb mixture in bottom of ungreased 9-inch square pan. Spoon filling mixture over crust, spreading evenly. Sprinkle with remaining crumb mixture.

5 Bake 45 to 55 minutes or until topping is golden brown and filling bubbles around edges. Cool slightly, about 10 minutes, before serving. Cut into 9 squares; top each serving with mound of frozen garnish.

High Altitude (3500–6500 ft): Heat oven to 350°F. In step 4, before adding filling and topping, prebake crust 12 minutes. In step 5, bake 50 to 55 minutes.

1 Serving: Calories 430 (Calories from Fat 140); Total Fat 15g (Saturated Fat 9g; Trans Fat 0.5g); Cholesterol 40mg; Sodium 90mg; Total Carbohydrate 69g (Dietary Fiber 4g; Sugars 45g); Protein 4g **% Daily Value:** Vitamin A 10%; Vitamin C 6%; Calcium 15%; Iron 10% **Exchanges:** 1 Starch, 3 $1/2$ Other Carbohydrate, 3 Fat **Carbohydrate Choices:** 4 $1/2$

cherry cream crunch

JOYCE HERR

Rogers, AR

Bake-Off® Contest 14 • New York City, 1962

12 SERVINGS

PREP TIME: *25 minutes*

START TO FINISH: *3 hours 15 minutes*

BASE AND TOPPING

1 cup all-purpose flour

$^1/_2$ cup packed brown sugar

$^1/_2$ teaspoon ground cinnamon

Dash salt

$^1/_2$ cup butter or margarine, softened

1 teaspoon vanilla

1 cup coconut

$^1/_2$ cup quick-cooking oats

$^1/_2$ cup chopped walnuts

FILLING

1 can (14 oz) sweetened condensed
milk (not evaporated)

1 tablespoon grated lemon peel

$^1/_4$ cup lemon juice

Dash salt

2 eggs, slightly beaten

1 can (21 oz) cherry or blueberry
pie filling

1 Heat oven to 375°F. In large bowl, beat flour, brown sugar, cinnamon, dash salt, the butter and vanilla with electric mixer on low speed until crumbly. Stir in coconut, oats and walnuts. Press 2 $^1/_2$ cups crumb mixture into bottom of ungreased 12 × 8-inch (2-quart) glass baking dish or 13 × 9-inch pan; reserve remaining crumb mixture for topping.

2 Bake base 12 minutes or until light golden brown. Meanwhile, in medium bowl, mix all filling ingredients except pie filling.

3 Spread filling evenly over partially baked base. Carefully spoon pie filling evenly over condensed milk mixture. Sprinkle reserved crumb mixture over top.

4 Bake 15 to 18 minutes longer or until top is golden brown. Cool 30 minutes. Refrigerate at least 2 hours before serving. Cut into squares. Store dessert in refrigerator.

High Altitude (3500–6500 ft): In step 2, bake base 14 minutes. In step 4, bake 19 to 22 minutes.

1 Serving: Calories 400 (Calories from Fat 160); Total Fat 18g (Saturated Fat 10g; Trans Fat 0.5g); Cholesterol 65mg; Sodium 160mg; Total Carbohydrate 54g (Dietary Fiber 2g; Sugars 41g); Protein 7g **% Daily Value:** Vitamin A 8%; Vitamin C 4%; Calcium 15%; Iron 8% **Exchanges:** 2 Starch, 1 $^1/_2$ Other Carbohydrate, 3 $^1/_2$ Fat **Carbohydrate Choices:** 3 $^1/_2$

black-bottom refrigerator dessert

6 SERVINGS

PREP TIME: *40 minutes*

START TO FINISH: *4 hours 25 minutes*

JACK JALVING

Kalamazoo, MI

Bake-Off® Contest 05 • New York City, 1953

1 Heat oven to 350°F. Generously grease 9-inch square pan with shortening; lightly flour. In 2-quart saucepan, heat $^1/_2$ cup shortening and the chocolate over low heat, stirring frequently, until melted and smooth. Remove from heat. Cool 15 minutes.

2 Meanwhile, in small bowl, mix flour, baking powder and $^1/_2$ teaspoon salt; set aside.

3 Into cooled melted chocolate mixture, stir 1 cup sugar and 1 teaspoon vanilla until smooth. Add 1 egg at a time, beating well after each, until blended. Gradually stir in flour mixture until well mixed. Spread in pan.

4 Bake 25 to 30 minutes or until toothpick inserted in center comes out clean. Cool completely, about 1 hour.

5 Meanwhile, in medium bowl, beat egg whites and $^1/_4$ teaspoon salt with electric mixer on high speed until soft peaks form. Gradually add $^1/_4$ cup sugar, beating well after each addition. Continue beating until stiff, glossy peaks form.

6 In 1-quart saucepan, sprinkle gelatin over cold water. Let stand 2 minutes to soften. Heat over low heat, stirring constantly, until gelatin is dissolved. Cool to lukewarm, about 5 minutes. Fold into egg white mixture.

7 In small bowl, beat whipping cream and 1 teaspoon vanilla on high speed until stiff peaks form. Fold whipped cream into egg white-gelatin mixture. Spread cream chiffon over cooled brownie layer. Refrigerate at least 2 hours before serving. Cut into squares. Store dessert in refrigerator.

High Altitude (3500–6500 ft): No change.

BROWNIE LAYER
$^1/_2$ cup shortening

2 oz unsweetened baking chocolate

$^3/_4$ cup all-purpose flour

$^1/_2$ teaspoon baking powder

$^1/_2$ teaspoon salt

1 cup sugar

1 teaspoon vanilla

2 eggs

CREAM CHIFFON
2 pasteurized egg whites

$^1/_4$ teaspoon salt

$^1/_4$ cup sugar

1 envelope unflavored gelatin

$^1/_4$ cup cold water

$^3/_4$ cup whipping cream

1 teaspoon vanilla

1 Serving: Calories 560 (Calories from Fat 300); Total Fat 33g (Saturated Fat 14g; Trans Fat 3g); Cholesterol 105mg; Sodium 390mg; Total Carbohydrate 58g (Dietary Fiber 2g; Sugars 43g); Protein 8g **% Daily Value:** Vitamin A 8%; Vitamin C 0%; Calcium 6%; Iron 15% **Exchanges:** 2 $^1/_2$ Starch, 1 $^1/_2$ Other Carbohydrate, 6 Fat **Carbohydrate Choices:** 4

marble-ous peanut butter dessert

FLORENCE STULL

Danville, OH

Bake-Off® Contest 21 • San Diego, 1970

15 SERVINGS

PREP TIME: *30 minutes*

START TO FINISH: *3 hours 10 minutes*

CRUST

¹/₂ cup packed brown sugar

¹/₂ cup peanut butter

¹/₄ cup butter or margarine, softened

1 cup all-purpose flour

FILLING

1 package (8 oz) cream cheese, softened

¹/₂ cup granulated sugar

¹/₄ cup peanut butter

1 teaspoon vanilla

2 pasteurized eggs

1 cup whipping cream, whipped, sweetened

1 cup semisweet chocolate chips

1 Heat oven to 350°F. In small bowl, beat brown sugar, ¹/₂ cup peanut butter and the butter with electric mixer on medium speed until light and fluffy. Beat in flour until crumbly. Sprinkle crumb mixture into ungreased 12 × 8-inch (2-quart) or 13 × 9-inch (3-quart) glass baking dish. Bake 10 to 15 minutes or until golden brown. Cool 10 minutes.

2 Reserve half of crumb mixture (about 1 cup) for topping. Lightly press remaining crumb mixture in bottom of baking dish.

3 In small bowl, beat cream cheese, granulated sugar, ¹/₄ cup peanut butter and the vanilla on medium speed until smooth and creamy. Add 1 egg at a time, beating well after each. Fold in whipped cream. Pour over crumb mixture in baking dish.

4 In 1-quart saucepan, melt chocolate chips over low heat, stirring frequently, until melted and smooth. Drizzle chocolate over cream cheese mixture. With table knife, gently cut through both mixtures to marble. Sprinkle with reserved crumb mixture; press in slightly. Freeze at least 2 hours or until serving time. Let stand at room temperature 15 minutes before serving. Cut into squares.

High Altitude (3500–6500 ft): No change.

1 Serving: Calories 370 (Calories from Fat 220); Total Fat 24g (Saturated Fat 12g; Trans Fat 0.5g); Cholesterol 70mg; Sodium 150mg; Total Carbohydrate 31g (Dietary Fiber 2g; Sugars 22g); Protein 7g **% Daily Value:** Vitamin A 10%; Vitamin C 0%; Calcium 4%; Iron 8% **Exchanges:** 2 Other Carbohydrate, 1 High-Fat Meat, 3 Fat **Carbohydrate Choices:** 2

peach and crescent dessert

DOLORES LAMMERS

Morris, MN

Bake-Off® Contest 27 • Boston, 1976

12 SERVINGS

PREP TIME: *10 minutes*

START TO FINISH: *35 minutes*

1 can (8 oz) refrigerated crescent
    dinner rolls

2 tablespoons butter or margarine,
    softened

1/2 cup coconut, if desired

1 cup sour cream

1 egg

1 can (28 oz) sliced peaches (2 cups),
    well drained

1/2 cup packed brown sugar

Vanilla ice cream or whipped cream,
    if desired

1 Heat oven to 350°F. Separate dough into 2 long rectangles; place in ungreased 13 × 9-inch pan. Press dough to cover bottom of pan, firmly pressing perforations to seal. Spread with butter; sprinkle with coconut.

2 Bake 5 to 7 minutes or until crust is very lightly browned. Meanwhile, in small bowl, beat sour cream and egg until well blended.

3 Arrange peach slices over partially baked crust. Pour sour cream mixture over peaches; sprinkle with brown sugar. Bake 22 to 25 minutes longer or until crust is golden brown. Cut into squares. Serve warm with ice cream. Store dessert in refrigerator.

High Altitude (3500–6500 ft): No change.

1 Serving: Calories 190 (Calories from Fat 90); Total Fat 10g (Saturated Fat 5g; Trans Fat 1g); Cholesterol 35mg; Sodium 180mg; Total Carbohydrate 21g (Dietary Fiber 1g; Sugars 14g); Protein 3g **% Daily Value:** Vitamin A 10%; Vitamin C 0%; Calcium 4%; Iron 4% **Exchanges:** 1 Starch, 1/2 Other Carbohydrate, 2 Fat **Carbohydrate Choices:** 1 1/2

praline crescent dessert

8 SERVINGS

PREP TIME: *30 minutes*

START TO FINISH: *50 minutes*

MARJORIE HOOPER

Lakeland, FL

Bake-Off® Contest 30 • San Antonio, 1982

1 Heat oven to 375°F. In 2-quart saucepan, melt butter over low heat. Add brown sugar; cook 2 minutes, stirring constantly. Add sour cream; cook 4 minutes, stirring occasionally. Remove from heat. Stir in cereal, pecans and coconut until evenly coated.

2 Separate dough into 8 triangles. Place each triangle in ungreased regular-size muffin cup; press dough to cover bottom and side of each cup.

3 In small bowl, beat cream cheese and powdered sugar until well blended. Spoon rounded teaspoonful into each cup; spread over bottom. Divide brown sugar mixture evenly into cups.

4 Bake 11 to 16 minutes or until deep golden brown. Serve warm or cool topped with whipped cream. Store desserts in refrigerator.

High Altitude (3500–6500 ft): For brown sugar mixture, decrease butter, brown sugar, chopped pecans and coconut to $^1/_4$ cup each; decrease sour cream to 1 tablespoon and crisp rice cereal to $^1/_2$ cup.

$^1/_3$ cup butter or margarine

$^1/_2$ cup packed brown sugar

3 tablespoons sour cream

1 cup crisp rice cereal

$^1/_2$ cup chopped pecans or nuts

$^1/_2$ cup coconut

1 can (8 oz) refrigerated crescent dinner rolls

1 package (3 oz) cream cheese, softened

2 tablespoons powdered sugar

Whipped cream, if desired

1 Serving: Calories 380 (Calories from Fat 230); Total Fat 25g (Saturated Fat 12g; Trans Fat 2g); Cholesterol 35mg; Sodium 360mg; Total Carbohydrate 33g (Dietary Fiber 1g; Sugars 20g); Protein 4g **% Daily Value:** Vitamin A 10%; Vitamin C 0%; Calcium 4%; Iron 8% **Exchanges:** 1 Starch, 1 Other Carbohydrate, 5 Fat **Carbohydrate Choices:** 2

pumpkin pie squares

JERRY D. BUSCH
Gladbrook, IL
Bake-Off® Contest 24 • Hollywood, 1973

12 SERVINGS

PREP TIME: *15 minutes*
START TO FINISH: *2 hours*

CRUST

- ³/₄ cup all-purpose flour
- ³/₄ cup quick-cooking or old-fashioned oats
- ¹/₂ to 1 cup chopped nuts
- ¹/₂ cup butter or margarine, softened
- 1 box (4-serving size) butterscotch pudding and pie filling mix (not instant)

FILLING

- 2 eggs
- 1 cup flaked or shredded coconut, if desired
- 1 ¹/₂ teaspoons pumpkin pie spice
- 1 can (15 oz) pumpkin (2 cups)
- 1 can (14 oz) sweetened condensed milk (not evaporated)

TOPPING, IF DESIRED

Whipped cream or vanilla ice cream

1 Heat oven to 350°F. In large bowl, mix all crust ingredients; press in bottom of ungreased 13 × 9-inch pan.

2 In same bowl, beat eggs. Stir in remaining filling ingredients until blended. Pour over crust.

3 Bake 35 to 45 minutes or until knife inserted in center comes out clean. Cool completely, about 1 hour. Cut into squares. Serve topped with whipped cream. Store dessert in refrigerator.

High Altitude (3500–6500 ft): Heat oven to 375°F. In step 1, prebake crust about 8 minutes. Pour filling over crust; bake 38 to 48 minutes.

See photo on page 129

1 Serving: Calories 320 (Calories from Fat 140); Total Fat 15g (Saturated Fat 7g; Trans Fat 0.5g); Cholesterol 65mg; Sodium 150mg; Total Carbohydrate 38g (Dietary Fiber 2g; Sugars 25g); Protein 7g **% Daily Value:** Vitamin A 130%; Vitamin C 2%; Calcium 10%; Iron 8% **Exchanges:** 1 ¹/₂ Starch, 1 Other Carbohydrate, 3 Fat **Carbohydrate Choices:** 2 ¹/₂

lemon meringue dessert squares

12 SERVINGS

PREP TIME: *30 minutes*
START TO FINISH: *3 hours*

TINA PRINCIPATO
West Roxbury, MA
Bake-Off® Contest 23 • Houston, 1972

1 Heat oven to 350°F. Grease 13 × 9-inch pan with shortening. In large bowl, beat cake mix, $^1/_2$ cup butter and the egg with electric mixer on low speed until crumbly. Press mixture in bottom of pan.

2 In 2-quart saucepan, mix 1 $^1/_3$ cups sugar, the cornstarch and salt. Gradually stir in water until smooth. Cook over medium heat, stirring constantly, until mixture boils. Remove from heat. Stir about $^1/_2$ cup of hot mixture into egg yolks; return egg mixture to saucepan. Cook until mixture is bubbly (mixture will be very thick). Remove from heat; stir in 2 tablespoons butter, lemon peel and lemon juice. Pour filling over crust.

3 In small bowl, beat egg whites and cream of tartar with mixer on medium speed about 1 minute or until soft peaks form. Add $^1/_2$ cup sugar 1 tablespoon at a time, beating on high speed until stiff peaks form and sugar is dissolved. Spread meringue over hot filling.

4 Bake 25 to 30 minutes or until meringue is golden brown. Cool 1 hour. Refrigerate at least 1 hour before serving. Cut into squares.

High Altitude (3500–6500 ft): Heat oven to 375°F.

CRUST

1 box (18.25 oz) yellow cake mix with pudding

$^1/_2$ cup butter or margarine

1 egg

FILLING

1 $^1/_3$ cups sugar

$^1/_2$ cup cornstarch

Dash salt

1 $^3/_4$ cups water

4 egg yolks, slightly beaten

2 tablespoons butter or margarine

2 tablespoons grated lemon peel

$^1/_2$ cup lemon juice

MERINGUE

4 egg whites

$^1/_4$ teaspoon cream of tartar

$^1/_2$ cup sugar

1 Serving: Calories 440 (Calories from Fat 140); Total Fat 16g (Saturated Fat 8g; Trans Fat 1g); Cholesterol 110mg; Sodium 410mg; Total Carbohydrate 71g (Dietary Fiber 0g; Sugars 57g); Protein 5g **% Daily Value:** Vitamin A 8%; Vitamin C 4%; Calcium 6%; Iron 6% **Exchanges:** 1 $^1/_2$ Starch, 3 Other Carbohydrate, 3 Fat **Carbohydrate Choices:** 5

almond-toffee-mocha squares

BEVERLY STARR
Nashville, AR
Bake-Off® Contest 41 • Hollywood, 2004

16 BARS

PREP TIME: *20 minutes*
START TO FINISH: *2 hours 50 minutes*

BROWNIES

1 box (19.5 oz) fudge toffee or
traditional fudge brownie mix

1 teaspoon instant coffee granules
or crystals

$^1/_2$ cup butter or margarine, melted

$^1/_4$ cup water

2 eggs

$^1/_2$ cup finely chopped toffee candy
bars (two 1.4-oz bars)

$^1/_2$ cup slivered almonds, toasted*

TOPPING

4 oz cream cheese, softened

$^1/_3$ cup packed brown sugar

1 teaspoon instant coffee granules
or crystals

1 $^1/_2$ cups whipping cream

1 teaspoon vanilla

1 cup chopped toffee candy bar
(four 1.4-oz bars)

$^1/_2$ cup slivered almonds, toasted*

1 Heat oven to 350°F. Grease bottom only of 13 × 9-inch pan with shortening or cooking spray. In large bowl, beat brownie mix, 1 teaspoon instant coffee, the butter, water and eggs with electric mixer on low speed 1 minute. Gently stir in $^1/_2$ cup chopped candy bars and $^1/_2$ cup almonds. Spread batter in pan.

2 Bake 24 to 28 minutes or until edges are firm. DO NOT OVERBAKE. Cool completely in pan on wire rack, about 1 hour.

3 In medium bowl, beat cream cheese, brown sugar and 1 teaspoon instant coffee with mixer on medium speed until smooth. On high speed, beat in whipping cream and vanilla until soft peaks form.

4 Spread cream cheese mixture over cooled brownies. Sprinkle 1 cup chopped candy bars and 1/2 cup almonds over top. Refrigerate at least 1 hour before serving. Cut into 4 rows by 4 rows. Store bars in refrigerator.

High Altitude (3500–6500 ft): Make brownies following High Altitude directions on box. Bake 28 to 32 minutes.

To toast almonds, bake uncovered in ungreased shallow pan in 350°F oven about 10 minutes, stirring occasionally, until golden brown.

1 Bar: Calories 440 (Calories from Fat 230); Total Fat 26g (Saturated Fat 13g; Trans Fat 1.5g); Cholesterol 80mg; Sodium 250mg; Total Carbohydrate 46g (Dietary Fiber 0g; Sugars 36g); Protein 5g **% Daily Value:** Vitamin A 15%; Vitamin C 0%; Calcium 8%; Iron 8% **Exchanges:** 1 $^1/_2$ Starch, 1 $^1/_2$ Other Carbohydrate, 5 Fat **Carbohydrate Choices:** 3

sour cream–apple squares

LUELLA MAKI

Ely, MN

Bake-Off® Contest 26 • San Francisco, 1975

12 SERVINGS

PREP TIME: *20 minutes*

START TO FINISH: *1 hour 30 minutes*

2 cups all-purpose flour

2 cups packed brown sugar

$^1/_2$ cup butter or margarine, softened

1 cup chopped nuts

1 to 2 teaspoons ground cinnamon

1 teaspoon baking soda

$^1/_2$ teaspoon salt

1 container (8 oz) sour cream

1 teaspoon vanilla

1 egg

2 cups finely chopped, peeled apples
(2 medium)

Whipped cream or vanilla ice cream,
if desired

1 Heat oven to 350°F. In large bowl, beat flour, brown sugar and butter with electric mixer on low speed until crumbly. Stir in nuts. Press 2 $^3/_4$ cups crumb mixture in bottom of ungreased 13 × 9-inch pan.

2 To remaining mixture, add cinnamon, baking soda, salt, sour cream, vanilla and egg; mix well. Stir in apples. Spoon evenly over crumb mixture in pan.

3 Bake 30 to 40 minutes or until toothpick inserted in center comes out clean. Cool 30 minutes. Cut into squares. Serve warm or cool with whipped cream. Store dessert in refrigerator.

High Altitude (3500–6500 ft): Heat oven to 375°F. Bake 25 to 35 minutes.

1 Serving: Calories 410 (Calories from Fat 170); Total Fat 18g (Saturated Fat 8g; Trans Fat 0.5g); Cholesterol 50mg; Sodium 290mg; Total Carbohydrate 57g (Dietary Fiber 2g; Sugars 38g); Protein 5g **% Daily Value:** Vitamin A 8%; Vitamin C 0%; Calcium 6%; Iron 10% **Exchanges:** 1 $^1/_2$ Starch, 2 Other Carbohydrate, 3 $^1/_2$ Fat **Carbohydrate Choices:** 4

swedish apple mini-dumplings

4 SERVINGS

PREP TIME: *20 minutes*
START TO FINISH: *1 hour 10 minutes*

STELLA RILEY BENDER
Colorado Springs, CO
Bake-Off® Contest 36 • San Diego, 1994

1 Heat oven to 375°F. Spray 8-inch square (2-quart) glass baking dish with cooking spray. In small bowl, mix brown sugar, cinnamon, cardamom and vanilla; set aside.

2 Remove pie crust from pouch; unroll on work surface. Spread butter over crust; sprinkle with brown sugar mixture. Cut crust into 8 wedges; place apple slice crosswise in center of each wedge. Starting with pointed end, fold crust wedge over apple; fold corners of wide end of wedge over apple, forming dumpling and sealing completely. Place seam side down and sides touching in baking dish. Sprinkle with raisins.

3 In 1-quart saucepan, heat apple juice, sugar and cinnamon candies to boiling over medium heat. Cook 1 minute, stirring frequently, until candies are melted. Carefully pour over dumplings.

4 Bake 30 to 40 minutes or until crust is light golden brown, apples are tender and sauce thickens. Cool 10 minutes before serving. Spoon dumplings into serving dishes; spoon sauce over dumplings. Serve warm with half-and-half.

High Altitude (3500–6500 ft): Bake 35 to 40 minutes.

$1/2$ cup packed brown sugar

$1/2$ teaspoon ground cinnamon

$1/4$ teaspoon ground cardamom

2 teaspoons vanilla

1 refrigerated pie crust (from 15-oz box), softened as directed on box

1 tablespoon butter or margarine, softened

1 small Granny Smith apple, peeled, cored and cut into 8 slices

$1/4$ cup raisins

1 $1/2$ cups apple juice

3 tablespoons sugar

2 tablespoons red cinnamon candies

$1/4$ cup half-and-half

1 Serving: Calories 540 (Calories from Fat 170); Total Fat 19g (Saturated Fat 8g; Trans Fat 0g); Cholesterol 20mg; Sodium 260mg; Total Carbohydrate 91g (Dietary Fiber 0g; Sugars 60g); Protein 0g **% Daily Value:** Vitamin A 4%; Vitamin C 0%; Calcium 6%; Iron 6% **Exchanges:** 6 Other Carbohydrate, 4 Fat **Carbohydrate Choices:** 6

zebra brownie doughnuts

ROSEMARY LEICHT

Bethel, OH

Bake-Off® Contest 40 • Orlando, 2002

12 DOUGHNUTS

PREP TIME: *20 minutes*

START TO FINISH: *40 minutes*

DOUGHNUTS

1 box (15.8 oz) double chocolate premium brownie mix with chocolate syrup

$1/2$ cup buttermilk*

$1/4$ cup light or extra-light olive oil

1 egg

GLAZE

1 $1/2$ cups powdered sugar

1 teaspoon vanilla

3 to 4 tablespoons milk

1 Heat oven to 400°F. Grease 12 nonstick miniature fluted tube cake cups (six 1-cup fluted cups per pan) with shortening.

2 Reserve chocolate syrup packet from brownie mix. In large bowl, beat brownie mix, buttermilk, oil and egg with electric mixer on medium speed 1 minute 30 seconds to 2 minutes or until smooth. Spoon 2 heaping measuring tablespoonfuls batter into each cup.

3 Bake 10 to 15 minutes or until toothpick inserted in center comes out clean. Cool 5 minutes. Run knife around edge of each doughnut to loosen. Remove from cups; place on wire rack.

4 In small bowl, blend all glaze ingredients until smooth, adding enough milk for desired glazing consistency. Brush or spoon glaze over fluted side of each doughnut. Cut off small corner from chocolate syrup packet; drizzle syrup over doughnuts.

High Altitude (3500–6500 ft): Add $1/4$ cup all-purpose flour to dry brownie mix.

*To substitute for buttermilk, use 1 $1/2$ teaspoons vinegar or lemon juice plus milk to make $1/2$ cup.

1 Doughnut: Calories 270 (Calories from Fat 80); Total Fat 9g (Saturated Fat 2.5g; Trans Fat 0.5g); Cholesterol 20mg; Sodium 110mg; Total Carbohydrate 45g (Dietary Fiber 1g; Sugars 37g); Protein 2g **% Daily Value:** Vitamin A 0%; Vitamin C 0%; Calcium 2%; Iron 6% **Exchanges:** 1 Starch, 2 Other Carbohydrate, 1 $1/2$ Fat **Carbohydrate Choices:** 3

raspberry-mango shortcakes

8 SHORTCAKES

PREP TIME: *50 minutes*

START TO FINISH: *50 minutes*

NANCY FLESCH

Kent, OH

Bake-Off® Contest 37 • Dallas, 1996

1 Heat oven to 375°F. In small bowl, mix coconut, $^1/_4$ cup granulated sugar and $^1/_2$ teaspoon ginger.

2 Separate dough into 8 biscuits. Dip top and sides of each biscuit into melted butter; dip top and sides into coconut mixture. Place biscuits, coconut side up, 2 inches apart on ungreased cookie sheet. Sprinkle any remaining coconut mixture over tops of biscuits.

3 Bake 14 to 18 minutes or until biscuits and coconut are light golden brown. Cool 5 minutes.

4 Meanwhile, in medium bowl, gently stir together all fruit mixture ingredients. In small bowl, beat all topping ingredients with electric mixer on high speed until stiff peaks form.

5 To serve, split warm biscuits; place bottom halves on dessert plates. Spoon generous $^1/_3$ cup fruit mixture over each biscuit half; top each with $^1/_4$ cup topping and biscuit top. Store fruit and topping in refrigerator.

High Altitude (3500–6500 ft): No change.

SHORTCAKES

$^1/_2$ cup coconut

$^1/_4$ cup granulated sugar

$^1/_2$ teaspoon ground ginger

1 can (16.3 oz) large refrigerated buttermilk homestyle biscuits

2 tablespoons butter or margarine, melted

FRUIT MIXTURE

2 cups fresh or frozen (partially thawed) raspberries

1 $^1/_2$ cups chopped peeled fresh mangoes or 1 jar or can (16 oz) mangoes or peaches, drained, chopped

2 tablespoons granulated sugar

TOPPING

1 cup whipping cream

2 tablespoons packed brown sugar

$^1/_4$ teaspoon ground ginger

1 Shortcake: Calories 420 (Calories from Fat 200); Total Fat 22g (Saturated Fat 12g; Trans Fat 3.5g); Cholesterol 40mg; Sodium 650mg; Total Carbohydrate 49g (Dietary Fiber 3g; Sugars 25g); Protein 5g **% Daily Value:** Vitamin A 15%; Vitamin C 30%; Calcium 6%; Iron 10% **Exchanges:** 1 $^1/_2$ Starch, $^1/_2$ Fruit, 1 Other Carbohydrate, 4 $^1/_2$ Fat **Carbohydrate Choices:** 3

granola "fried" ice cream with red cinnamon sauce

JAN PERRY

Norwood, NC

Bake-Off® Contest 41 • Hollywood, 2004

8 SERVINGS

PREP TIME: *35 minutes*

START TO FINISH: *45 minutes*

FRIED ICE CREAM

2 pints (4 cups) vanilla ice cream

1 cup butter or margarine

1 box (8.9 oz) cinnamon crunchy granola bars (12 bars), crushed*

1 cup finely chopped pecans

SAUCE

$1/2$ cup sugar

$1/2$ cup water

$1/2$ cup red cinnamon candies (4 $1/2$ oz)

1 Line plate or tray with waxed paper. Scoop ice cream into 8 ($1/2$-cup) balls onto paper-lined plate; place in freezer until hard, about 30 minutes.

2 Meanwhile, in 12-inch skillet, melt butter over medium heat. Add crushed granola bars and pecans; cook 3 to 5 minutes, stirring constantly, until deep golden brown and most of butter is absorbed (mixture will look foamy). Spread in 13 × 9-inch pan; cool completely, about 20 minutes.

3 In 1-quart saucepan, heat all sauce ingredients over medium-high heat, stirring constantly, just until mixture boils. Reduce heat to medium-low; simmer uncovered 4 to 5 minutes, stirring frequently, until candies melt. Remove from heat. Pour sauce into glass measuring cup. Cool 10 minutes.

4 Working quickly, remove 1 ice cream ball at a time from freezer; roll ball in crumb mixture, pressing mixture into ball until completely covered. Return to freezer until ready to serve.

5 To serve, spoon 1 tablespoon cooled sauce onto each dessert plate. Place coated ice cream balls over sauce. Drizzle each with 1 tablespoon sauce, letting some run down sides (reheat sauce slightly if too thick to drizzle). Serve immediately.

High Altitude (3500–6500 ft): No change.

To easily crush granola bars, do not unwrap; use rolling pin to crush bars.

1 Serving: Calories 700 (Calories from Fat 410); Total Fat 45g (Saturated Fat 21g; Trans Fat 1.5g); Cholesterol 95mg; Sodium 350mg; Total Carbohydrate 65g (Dietary Fiber 3g; Sugars 48g); Protein 7g **% Daily Value:** Vitamin A 20%; Vitamin C 0%; Calcium 10%; Iron 6% **Exchanges:** 1 Starch, 3 Other Carbohydrate, $1/2$ Low-Fat Milk, 8 $1/2$ Fat **Carbohydrate Choices:** 4

peaches 'n cream supreme

GAIL E. TAVCAR
Lyndhurst, OH
Bake-Off® Contest 22 • Honolulu, 1971

8 SERVINGS
PREP TIME: *25 minutes*
START TO FINISH: *3 hours 30 minutes*

FILLING
- $^1/_3$ cup granulated sugar
- $^1/_4$ teaspoon salt
- $^1/_4$ cup sour cream
- 1 package (3 oz) cream cheese, softened
- 1 egg

CRUST
- 1 cup all-purpose flour
- $^2/_3$ cup granulated sugar
- 1 teaspoon baking powder
- $^1/_4$ teaspoon salt
- $^1/_2$ cup butter or margarine, softened
- Reserved 1 tablespoon peach liquid (from can of peaches)
- 1 teaspoon vanilla
- 2 eggs

TOPPING
- 1 can (29 oz) sliced peaches, drained, 1 tablespoon liquid reserved
- 1 cup sour cream
- $^1/_4$ cup packed brown sugar

1 Heat oven to 350°F. Grease bottom and side of 9-inch deep-dish or 10-inch pie plate. In small bowl, beat all filling ingredients with electric mixer on medium speed about 3 minutes or until smooth and creamy; set aside.

2 In large bowl, beat all crust ingredients on medium speed until smooth, scraping bowl occasionally. Spread batter evenly in bottom and up side of pie plate. Pour filling into crust-lined pie plate.

3 Bake 25 to 30 minutes or until crust is light golden brown.

4 Top with peach slices. In small bowl, mix 1 cup sour cream and the brown sugar; spoon over peaches. Bake 5 minutes longer. Cool on wire rack 30 minutes. Refrigerate at least 2 hours before serving.

High Altitude (3500–6500 ft): Bake 30 to 35 minutes.

1 Serving: Calories 450 (Calories from Fat 220); Total Fat 24g (Saturated Fat 15g; Trans Fat 1g); Cholesterol 145mg; Sodium 370mg; Total Carbohydrate 52g (Dietary Fiber 2g; Sugars 38g); Protein 6g **% Daily Value:** Vitamin A 30%; Vitamin C 2%; Calcium 10%; Iron 10% **Exchanges:** 2 Starch, 1 $^1/_2$ Other Carbohydrate, 4 $^1/_2$ Fat **Carbohydrate Choices:** 3 $^1/_2$

crescent-macadamia truffle cups

GLORIA PLEASANTS
Williamsburg, VA
Bake-Off® Contest 34 • Phoenix, 1990

24 TRUFFLE CUPS

PREP TIME: *40 minutes*
START TO FINISH: *4 hours*

FILLING AND CRUST

4 oz sweet baking chocolate, chopped

1/4 cup unsalted butter, regular butter or margarine

1/4 cup packed brown sugar

2 tablespoons all-purpose flour

2 tablespoons coffee-flavored liqueur or cold brewed coffee

1 egg

1 can (8 oz) refrigerated crescent dinner rolls

24 whole macadamia nuts

TOPPING

3 oz white chocolate baking bar, chopped

1/3 cup cream cheese spread (from 8-oz container)

1/2 cup whipping cream

2 tablespoons powdered sugar

1 teaspoon vanilla

1 Heat oven to 350°F. In 1-quart saucepan, melt sweet chocolate and butter over low heat, stirring constantly, until smooth. Remove from heat. Stir in brown sugar, flour, liqueur and egg; set aside.

2 Unroll dough into 2 long rectangles; firmly press perforations to seal. Cut each rectangle in half lengthwise. Cut each half crosswise into 6 (2-inch) squares. Press or roll out each square to 2 3/4-inch square. Place 1 square in each of 24 ungreased mini muffin cups; firmly press in bottom and up side, leaving corners of dough extended over edge of each cup.

3 Place 1 macadamia nut in each dough-lined cup. Spoon about 2 teaspoons filling mixture over nut in each cup.

4 Bake 12 to 15 minutes or until filling is set and corners of dough are golden brown. Cool 5 minutes. Remove from pan; place on wire racks. Cool completely, about 30 minutes. Refrigerate until thoroughly chilled, about 1 hour.

5 In 1-quart saucepan, melt white baking bar and cream cheese over low heat, stirring constantly, until smooth. Cover with plastic wrap; refrigerate until thoroughly chilled, about 1 hour, stirring occasionally.

6 In small bowl, beat whipping cream, powdered sugar and vanilla with electric mixer on high speed just until soft peaks form. Add chilled white baking bar mixture; beat on low speed just until well blended. Pipe or spoon topping over top of chilled cups. Refrigerate until topping is set, about 30 minutes. Store truffle cups in refrigerator.

High Altitude (3500–6500 ft): No change.

1 Truffle Cup: Calories 160 (Calories from Fat 100); Total Fat 12g (Saturated Fat 6g; Trans Fat 0.5g); Cholesterol 25mg; Sodium 150mg; Total Carbohydrate 12g (Dietary Fiber 1g; Sugars 7g); Protein 2g **% Daily Value:** Vitamin A 4%; Vitamin C 0%; Calcium 2%; Iron 8% **Exchanges:** 1/2 Starch, 1/2 Other Carbohydrate, 2 Fat **Carbohydrate Choices:** 1

banana dessert wraps

4 SERVINGS

PREP TIME: *20 minutes*
START TO FINISH: *40 minutes*

HEATHER SNEDIC
Lisle, IL
Bake-Off® Contest 41 • Hollywood, 2004

1 Heat oven to 350°F. Spread coconut and pecans separately on cookie sheet. Bake 5 to 8 minutes, stirring occasionally, until light golden brown; set aside.

2 Increase oven temperature to 450°F. Remove pie crust from pouch; unroll on work surface. With rolling pin, roll crust until 12 inches in diameter.

3 In small bowl, mix sugar, cinnamon and nutmeg. Reserve 1 tablespoon sugar mixture; sprinkle remaining sugar mixture evenly over crust. Cut crust into 4 wedge-shaped pieces.

4 Place 1 banana lengthwise on each crust wedge, about $3/4$ inch from curved edge (if banana is too long, trim ends so it fits within crust, at least $1/4$ inch from each edge). Push about 1 rounded tablespoon chocolate chips, points first, into top and sides of each banana.

5 Bring curved edge and point of each crust wedge up over banana to meet; pinch seam and ends to seal, shaping crust around banana. Sprinkle tops of wrapped bananas with reserved 1 tablespoon sugar mixture; place on ungreased cookie sheet.

6 Bake 10 to 14 minutes or until golden brown. Immediately remove from cookie sheet. Cool 5 minutes.

7 To serve, drizzle or spread about 2 tablespoons warm caramel topping on each dessert plate. Top each with baked banana, whipped cream and if desired, additional caramel topping. Sprinkle coconut and pecans over top of each. Serve with ice cream.

High Altitude (3500–6500 ft): After toasting coconut and pecans, increase oven temperature to 425°F. In step 6, bake wrapped bananas 15 to 19 minutes.

$1/2$ cup coconut

$1/2$ cup chopped pecans

1 refrigerated pie crust (from 15-oz box), softened as directed on box

$1/4$ cup sugar

$1/2$ teaspoon ground cinnamon

$1/4$ teaspoon ground nutmeg

4 firm ripe bananas (5 to 6 inch)

$1/3$ cup semisweet chocolate chips

1 jar (12 oz) hot caramel topping, heated

Whipped cream, if desired

1 cup vanilla ice cream

1 Serving: Calories 940 (Calories from Fat 330); Total Fat 37g (Saturated Fat 15g; Trans Fat 0g); Cholesterol 25mg; Sodium 580mg; Total Carbohydrate 147g (Dietary Fiber 7g; Sugars 88g); Protein 6g **% Daily Value:** Vitamin A 6%; Vitamin C 10%; Calcium 10%; Iron 10% **Exchanges:** 2 Starch, 2 Fruit, 5 Other Carbohydrate, 7 Fat **Carbohydrate Choices:** 10

thick 'n fudgy triple-chocolate pudding cake

JANICE KOLLAR

Woodbridge, NJ

Bake-Off® Contest 39 • San Francisco, 2000

9 SERVINGS

PREP TIME: *15 minutes*

START TO FINISH: *1 hour 30 minutes*

---

1 box (15.8 oz) double chocolate premium brownie mix with chocolate syrup

$1/2$ teaspoon baking powder

$1/2$ cup milk

$1/4$ cup butter or margarine, melted

1 teaspoon vanilla

1 $1/2$ cups water

1 $1/2$ teaspoons instant espresso coffee granules

1 cup chocolate fudge creamy ready-to-spread frosting (from 1-lb container)

Whipped cream or vanilla ice cream

1 Heat oven to 350°F. Spray 9- or 8-inch square pan with cooking spray. In large bowl, mix brownie mix and baking powder. Stir in milk, butter, vanilla and chocolate syrup from packet in brownie mix. Spread batter in pan.

2 In 2-quart saucepan, heat water to boiling. Add espresso granules; stir to dissolve. Add frosting; cook over low heat, stirring frequently, until melted and smooth. Slowly pour over batter in pan. DO NOT STIR.

3 Bake 40 to 45 minutes or until edges are bubbly and cake begins to pull away from sides of pan (top may appear shiny in spots). Cool 30 minutes before serving. Serve warm or cold with whipped cream. Store cake in refrigerator.

High Altitude (3500–6500 ft): Add $1/3$ cup all-purpose flour to dry brownie mix; decrease water to 1 cup.

1 Serving: Calories 410 (Calories from Fat 160); Total Fat 18g (Saturated Fat 11g; Trans Fat 1g); Cholesterol 15mg; Sodium 200mg; Total Carbohydrate 59g (Dietary Fiber 2g; Sugars 46g); Protein 3g **% Daily Value:** Vitamin A 4%; Vitamin C 0%; Calcium 4%; Iron 10% **Exchanges:** 1 Starch, 3 Other Carbohydrate, 3 $1/2$ Fat **Carbohydrate Choices:** 4

pineapple galette with caramel-rum sauce

Great Falls, MT
Bake-Off® Contest 37 • Dallas, 1996

8 SERVINGS
PREP TIME: *15 minutes*
START TO FINISH: *1 hour 20 minutes*

CRUST
1 refrigerated pie crust (from 15-oz box), softened as directed on box

TOPPING
1/4 cup all-purpose flour

2 tablespoons granulated sugar

3 tablespoons brown sugar

1/2 teaspoon ground ginger

1/2 teaspoon ground cinnamon

1/8 teaspoon ground nutmeg

1/4 cup butter or margarine, cut into pieces

1/4 cup finely chopped macadamia nuts

1 can (8 oz) crushed pineapple, drained

1 can (15 1/4 oz) pineapple slices, drained, cut in half

SAUCE
1 cup caramel topping

1/2 cup coarsely chopped macadamia nuts

1 tablespoon rum or 1 teaspoon rum extract, if desired

1. Heat oven to 375°F. Remove pie crust from pouch; unroll on ungreased cookie sheet.

2. In medium bowl, mix flour, sugar, brown sugar, ginger, cinnamon and nutmeg. With pastry blender or fork, cut in butter until mixture resembles coarse crumbs. Stir in 1/4 cup macadamia nuts.

3. Sprinkle half of the crumb mixture over crust to within 1 inch of edge. Top with crushed pineapple and halved pineapple slices. Sprinkle with remaining crumb mixture. Fold in pie crust edge 1 inch to form border; flute.

4. Bake 25 to 35 minutes or until crust is golden brown. Cool 30 minutes.

5. Meanwhile, in 1-quart saucepan, heat caramel topping over low heat, stirring occasionally, until warm. Stir in 1/2 cup macadamia nuts and the rum. Cut warm galette into 8 wedges; place on dessert plates. Spoon 2 tablespoons warm sauce over each serving.

High Altitude (3500–6500 ft): Bake 33 to 38 minutes.

1 Serving: Calories 450 (Calories from Fat 190); Total Fat 21g (Saturated Fat 7g; Trans Fat 0g); Cholesterol 20mg; Sodium 320mg; Total Carbohydrate 64g (Dietary Fiber 2g; Sugars 40g); Protein 2g **% Daily Value:** Vitamin A 6%; Vitamin C 6%; Calcium 4%; Iron 6% **Exchanges:** 1/2 Starch, 3 1/2 Other Carbohydrate, 4 Fat **Carbohydrate Choices:** 4

helpful nutrition information

Nutrition Guidelines

We provide nutrition information for each recipe that includes calories, fat, cholesterol, sodium, carbohydrate, fiber and protein. Individual food choices can be based on this information.

Recommended intake for a daily diet of 2,000 calories as set by the Food and Drug Administration

Total Fat	Less than 65g
Saturated Fat	Less than 20g
Cholesterol	Less than 300mg
Sodium	Less than 2,400mg
Total Carbohydrate	300g
Dietary Fiber	25g

Criteria Used for Calculating Nutrition Information

- The first ingredient was used wherever a choice is given (such as $1/3$ cup sour cream or plain yogurt).
- The first ingredient amount was used wherever a range is given (such as 3- to 3-$1/2$–pound cut-up broiler-fryer chicken).
- The first serving number was used wherever a range is given (such as 4 to 6 servings).
- "If desired" ingredients and recipe variations were not included (such as sprinkle with brown sugar, if desired).
- Only the amount of a marinade or frying oil that is estimated to be absorbed by the food during preparation or cooking was calculated.

Ingredients Used in Recipe Testing and Nutrition Calculations

- Ingredients used for testing represent those that the majority of consumers use in their homes: large eggs, 2% milk, 80%-lean ground beef, canned ready-to-use chicken broth and vegetable oil spread containing not less than 65% fat.
- Fat-free, low-fat or low-sodium products were not used, unless otherwise indicated.
- Solid vegetable shortening (not butter, margarine, non-stick cooking sprays or vegetable oil spread as they can cause sticking problems) was used to grease pans, unless otherwise indicated.

Equipment Used in Recipe Testing

We use equipment for testing that the majority of consumers use in their homes. If a specific piece of equipment (such as a wire whisk) is necessary for recipe success, it is listed in the recipe.

- Cookware and bakeware without nonstick coatings were used, unless otherwise indicated.
- No dark-colored, black or insulated bakeware was used.
- When a pan is specified in a recipe, a metal pan was used; a baking dish or pie plate means ovenproof glass was used.
- An electric hand mixer was used for mixing only when mixer speeds are specified in the recipe directions. When a mixer speed is not given, a spoon or fork was used.

Volume

U.S. Units	Canadian Metric	Australian Metric
1/4 teaspoon	1 mL	1 ml
1/2 teaspoon	2 mL	2 ml
1 teaspoon	5 mL	5 ml
1 tablespoon	15 mL	20 ml
1/4 cup	50 mL	60 ml
1/3 cup	75 mL	80 ml
1/2 cup	125 mL	125 ml
2/3 cup	150 mL	170 ml
3/4 cup	175 mL	190 ml
1 cup	250 mL	250 ml
1 quart	1 liter	1 liter
1 1/2 quarts	1.5 liters	1.5 liters
2 quarts	2 liters	2 liters
2 1/2 quarts	2.5 liters	2.5 liters
3 quarts	3 liters	3 liters
4 quarts	4 liters	4 liters

Weight

U.S. Units	Canadian Metric	Australian Metric
1 ounce	30 grams	30 grams
2 ounces	55 grams	60 grams
3 ounces	85 grams	90 grams
4 ounces (1/4 pound)	115 grams	125 grams
8 ounces (1/2 pound)	225 grams	225 grams
16 ounces (1 pound)	455 grams	500 grams
1 pound	455 grams	1/2 kilogram

Measurements

Inches	Centimeters
1	2.5
2	5.0
3	7.5
4	10.0
5	12.5
6	15.0
7	17.5
8	20.5
9	23.0
10	25.5
11	28.0
12	30.5
13	33.0

Temperatures

Fahrenheit	Celsius
32°	0°
212°	100°
250°	120°
275°	140°
300°	150°
325°	160°
350°	180°
375°	190°
400°	200°
425°	220°
450°	230°
475°	240°
500°	260°

Note: The recipes in this cookbook have not been developed or tested using metric measures. When converting recipes to metric, some variations in quality may be noted.

index

Page numbers in *italics* indicate illustrations.